DATE DUE

MEDIA

TEACHING SOCIAL MEDIA

The Can-Do Guide

Liz Kirchhoff

LIBRARIES UNLIMITED

AN IMPRINT OF ABC-CLIO, LLC
Santa Barbara, California • Denver, Colorado • Oxford, England

Library of Congress Cataloging-in-Publication Data

Kirchhoff, Liz.
  Teaching social media : the can-do guide / Liz Kirchhoff.
    pages cm
  Includes index.
    ISBN 978–1–61069–556–5 (pbk : alk. paper) — ISBN 978–1–61069–557–2 (ebook)
1. Libraries and adult education—Case studies.   2. Social media—Study and teaching.
3. Online social networks—Study and teaching.   I. Title.
Z718.8.K57 2014
006.7′54071—dc23   2014015854

ISBN: 978–1–61069–556–5
EISBN: 978–1–61069–557–2

18 17 16 15 14   1 2 3 4 5

This book is also available on the World Wide Web as an eBook.
Visit www.abc-clio.com for details.

Libraries Unlimited
An Imprint of ABC-CLIO, LLC

ABC-CLIO, LLC
130 Cremona Drive, P.O. Box 1911
Santa Barbara, California 93116-1911

This book is printed on acid-free paper ∞

Manufactured in the United States of America

CONTENTS

Introduction   vii

1. Twitter   1

2. Foursquare   15

3. Yelp   21

4. Pinterest   29

5. Facebook   39

6. LinkedIn   71

7. Google+   87

8. Other Social Media   103

Conclusion   115

Index   117

INTRODUCTION

Unless you've been living under a rock for the past decade, you know about such social media sites as Facebook, LinkedIn, and Pinterest—and so do your library customers. Chances are, you're getting questions about these sites—e.g., "How do I use LinkedIn to find a job?" and "How can I post photos on my Facebook page?"

Librarians, and especially public librarians, are increasingly being thrust into the position of helping their patrons with new technologies. This presents libraries with a great opportunity to better serve their communities; and because of this growing demand, many librarians have begun offering classes, which can be a more efficient and thorough approach to helping people with their tech needs. But, if you haven't previously taught classes or don't feel completely confident of your knowledge of social media, the idea of teaching a class can be intimidating, to say the least. That's where this book comes in—it offers you an outline of what to cover, along with sample scripts on presenting, and reproducible handouts to distribute to class participants. It is intended for those who may be new to teaching or new to social media, as well as those who have more experience but are looking for support or new ideas.

WHAT IS SOCIAL MEDIA?

Social media is a rapidly expanding group of websites and apps that facilitate connections between people around the world. These are almost all fully interactive, which has led to a focus on creating media instead of just consuming it. There are hundreds and hundreds of social media sites and apps. Some we all know (Facebook, Twitter, LinkedIn), while others are for a more niche audience. Still others fold under as quickly as they appear on the scene. There's an incredibly variety of topics, too! We have social networking sites like Facebook, Twitter, and Google+; gaming sites like World of Warcraft and Second Life; book sites like Goodreads, Shelfari, and LibraryThing; music sites like Pandora, Last.fm, and Spotify; productivity tools like Evernote, Google Drive, and Dropbox; knowledge-sharing sites like Wikipedia; photography sites like Flickr and Instagram; blogging sites like WordPress, Blogger, Tumblr, and LiveJournal; crafting sites like Ravelry and Etsy; networking sites like LinkedIn; and much, much more.

Most social media can be accessed via either website or mobile app. It's increasingly common that apps are just as robust as the website. Foursquare and Instagram are two great examples of this. As the line between mobile and website blurs, we'll probably see many more people who access social media strictly on mobile apps. As an educator, you'll want to consider this as you prepare your classes. If the technology is available to you, it is incredibly valuable to teach apps as well as websites.

WHY SOCIAL MEDIA IN THE LIBRARY?

This can be a real hot-button issue for some libraries and workplaces. Many places still block social media websites with the rationale that they are productivity killers. It can be tough to argue against this, as it can be true. Thankfully, as these sites become more mainstream, more places are now embracing social media to some extent.

So, why teach social media in the library? There are a lot of reasons for this, but our biggest reason should be that our patrons are using it and need our help. Libraries are not format specific; it is our job to help people find information on anything that they need to know. As more and more of the world moves to social media and networking, we risk becoming less relevant and less helpful to our patrons if we cannot help them learn to use it.

It is also becoming increasingly important that job applicants be comfortable with social media and other Internet websites. Many hiring managers now actively look for a presence on social media sites when considering applicants. Having these skills can vastly improve your chances of getting a job in this extremely difficult climate.

Within the past few years, there has been a significant trend toward creating content instead of just consuming it. This stems directly from social media websites, and many libraries have risen admirably to the challenge with creation spaces. These usually include a top-of-the-line computer with advanced video and sound editing programs, video cameras, green screens, scanners, and lots more. The final products can be saved to hard drives, but are just as frequently uploaded to YouTube, Flickr, or other media-sharing sites. Many schools are now assigning content creation as an important part of their curriculum, too.

HOW DO YOU GET ADMINISTRATIVE
APPROVAL AND STAFF BUY-IN?

Let's start with administration. You can argue a few things here. First, you might do an informal survey of libraries near you to determine what social media is being taught and where. Most libraries seem to be at least teaching Facebook now. The argument that most libraries in your area are teaching at least some social media can be powerful. Be sure to bring numbers and names to your employer.

Second, you might argue that since more and more people are now using social media for a wider variety of things, it is essential that it be taught in your libraries. For example, you might mention the fact that more and more prospective employers are now requiring at least some familiarity with social media. Perhaps you could integrate Facebook and LinkedIn classes with your current job searching resources.

If you're feeling bold and things are going well, you might suggest teaching social media as a part of creating a social media presence for the library. You could start with Facebook and Twitter. Both are incredibly fast and easy to set up and take only a few minutes a day to maintain. They're fabulous, free marketing for your library, and every library should have a page.

Finally, create a strategy. Decide generally how often you'd like to teach and for how long. Talk about what you'd like to cover, and what you hope the outcome will be. Bring this book and show your supervisor the adaptable handouts. The fact that you won't need to spend a lot of staff time creating a curriculum and handouts is a distinct benefit, especially for time and cash-strapped libraries.

Once you've received permission from your administration, you'll be ready to start working with staff at your library. At our library, we started with one-on-one and group classes for staff. Don't make it a requirement for people to create an account, since many just aren't that comfortable. Do make yourself accessible for questions and suggestions. Consider how what you're teaching can benefit your coworkers as well as your library. Since you know your coworkers, you should be able to tailor your classes somewhat to appeal to their interests. And remember, despite your best efforts, it may take some time for people to accept social media in their workplace. Be patient and enthusiastic and most people will come around eventually.

WHERE TO START

Start with what you're comfortable with. If you love Facebook, start by teaching that. If you're more of a Twitter fan, that's the place to start. It's much less scary to start with something you know.

If you're feeling unsure, perhaps you could begin with some one-on-one appointments. Pay attention to the questions you are asked, and let those be the foundation for what you teach. Copy the handouts in this book, and use the Instructor Notes as a place to begin. Remember, these can be edited or enhanced to fit your class needs at any time.

PREPARE YOURSELF

There are hundreds of resources online to teach yourself how to use social media and keep up with emerging trends. Some of the best places to begin include *Wired* magazine, Gizmodo, TechCrunch, and Mashable. If your library has Atomic Learning, that resource covers some social networking sites with step-by-step videos. YouTube is also a great source, especially for very specific questions. Just search your topic for a list of videos. Be sure to note the date on the video. Social media changes extremely quickly, so a video older than a few months will probably already be out of date.

It's easy to get overwhelmed trying to keep up with the utter deluge of information on the various tech sites. Over the years, I've learned to scan as much as possible and read relatively little. When looking at these types of blogs, it's often best to look for trends. What is being frequently mentioned? Is it anything that could be helpful to you? You need to be selective, since you can't possibly read it all.

As you might imagine, the best way to prepare for your classes is to actually use the website and app that you're teaching as much as possible. It can be extremely difficult to teach something that you yourself aren't that comfortable with. Familiarize yourself enough to be able to comfortably answer questions on a variety of topics. You should be able to navigate quickly to just about any page. It's okay to not know the answer every time, as long as you know generally where to look to figure it out. You can come back to questions later in class, too, as well as email or call your patron with the answer at a later time.

PLAN THE CONTENT, BUT REMAIN FLEXIBLE

By using a book like this, you will already have a leg up on planning for your class. Use the included handouts as a handy way to start. Feel free to cut content or embellish to fit the needs of your class. More on this later.

The content you cover will depend on your class. The ability level that you start with will be key, as well as knowing how much time you have. If you are a public librarian, your reality is likely that you often won't know these things until the students show up. As you teach, adjust accordingly. If you're teaching a class on Facebook and it's really clear that your class hasn't used it at all before, you could probably teach the features that they'll use on a daily basis, as well as walk through the privacy settings. Be really careful about not overwhelming your students. This can be tough when there's so much to cover.

DECIDE ON THE FORMAT

This is one of the most important questions to consider as you're preparing your class. First of all, should the topic be taught as a class, or would it be better to do a one-on-one? Most topics actually benefit from having a full class. Often it's easier to go through an entire website with a full class, especially if you're doing a "tour" of it. Students often teach each other—and you—something you didn't know. This should happen, and you should welcome it. On the other hand, sometimes one-on-one appointments are best. Many business classes (such as Etsy for Businesses and Business Facebook) are more effectively taught in this way since you're able to give tailored advice and help your patron set up the page or service they need. In addition, if you have time to offer them, patrons who are absolute computer beginners really appreciate one-on-one appointments, since they often get lost in a large class. This is better for you, too, since you don't have to deal with such a large learning curve in a big group. Finally, some learning is best done in private. For example, at my library, we do one-on-one interviews to review and update Facebook privacy settings for patrons. These are particularly scary, and people really appreciate this service.

If you choose to teach the material as a full class, consider whether you would like it to be a demonstration, or hands-on. Demonstration classes are a great option when the website is distracting (Pinterest or Etsy), when it's a business class you've chosen to teach to a larger group, or if you have more than about 20 people. It can also be helpful to teach a class as a demonstration if you have a great deal of information that you need to convey quickly. Alternatively, hands-on classes are a terrific choice when teaching about websites that patrons need to practice on, or those that your patrons will probably have many questions about.

Consider the length of your class. For most, it seems like the sweet spot is an hour or so. Shorter, and your patrons tend to miss important elements; longer, and people lose interest. If you choose to teach a class for a longer session (maybe you decide to do a half-day Facebook class, for example) plan to give breaks at least hourly. Stop frequently for questions, and encourage folks who need to leave early to do so.

DETAILS

There are many other details to consider. Do you want to have a syllabus or course outline? Patrons love them and they can be great for classes where the content does not change frequently. Unfortunately, they can be difficult for social media classes, especially those that change quickly such as Facebook. Because these sites update and change constantly, it can be very difficult to keep a syllabus up to date. For these types of classes, you may save yourself some time by keeping a "tips and tricks" sheet to give out instead of a syllabus. These can include helpful advice as well as lists of interesting people and things to look for, and they can provide a quick cheat sheet. They're a terrific tool for the instructor since they rarely need updating and can be used in multiple versions of a class.

LIVE TOUR VERSUS POWERPOINT

Another important consideration when planning your class is whether you choose to teach a class live through going step by step on the Internet; or via screenshots in a PowerPoint presentation. Lots of teachers prefer to teach with PowerPoint, since it's predictable and easy to use. I've never taught this way, choosing instead to do virtual tours of the websites in question. Students respond well either way—I simply choose this method because it makes it easier to answer questions and tailor the class to the students.

Some libraries are now experimenting with using services like Google Hangouts to record and live-stream classes. This is a great idea! Each session is automatically archived to YouTube, so your patrons can watch it anytime. Over time, the collection of instructional videos you build up could be invaluable. All you need to start is a Google account and a camera.

TONE

As an instructor, the most important thing for you to do is to set the tone. You want students to understand that they cannot possibly ask a stupid question. You want them to feel comfortable interrupting to ask about anything they might not understand. Consider giving your business card to every single person who takes a class with you, and encourage them to contact you if they have any questions or need any help. This is what I do; and I frequently get follow-up appointments and questions. These gestures are important, since they are the building blocks to a better relationship with patrons. Many patrons come back to me over and over for questions on a wide variety of topics. I love that this happens, and I do everything possible to encourage it.

To set the tone, be as casual as possible. Be accessible and easygoing. To this end, start the class by giving a bit of information about yourself. Ask the class to interrupt you at any time with any question. People are often intimidated by social media, and keeping the class as light and casual as possible helps assuage their fears. You want to encourage them to play, and to try things out. They need to understand that they can't break anything!

As you're presenting, repeat things as many times as it takes. Patrons sometimes lose you, so it's important to stop often to ask if everyone is keeping up, and if anyone has any questions.

ASSESSING YOUR AUDIENCE

Assessing your audience can be tricky, but it's a really important thing to do. Generally, you can expect to have a completely mixed bag in a social media class. Skill level can and does range anywhere from a complete beginner to someone who knows even more than you do. One of the trickiest things is to keep the expert engaged while bringing the beginner up to speed. Be prepared—a lot of these students aren't even comfortable checking their email, much less setting up a Facebook account. They may need some hand-holding. In my experience, those that already know or have learned how to do something will play online while the beginners get caught up. Generally it will become apparent almost immediately what type of class you're working with. Just be flexible and willing to adjust the material that you are planning to cover based on what the class can do.

For example, you might have a Facebook class that is made up almost entirely of beginners. In a case like that, you may only want to go over the most vital Facebook functions with the class, and then walk through privacy settings. More advanced classes can get more content in between (like photos, groups, etc.). There's nothing wrong with this! You can give out your business card and offer to sit down individually with anyone who has questions that aren't answered in the class.

GENERAL INFORMATION FOR ALL CLASSES

Some information must be discussed in every class. You'll find out more about this in the coming chapters, but these are things that must be at least touched on. For example, you must always talk about privacy issues. You will almost certainly want to discuss what to share and what to avoid. For some classes (like Pinterest and Tumblr), you'll always want to take a quick moment to talk about copyright and fair use, and to explain that these sites could possibly be impermanent. Finally, you should also always take the time to promote the way your library is using something. If there's a library Twitter or Facebook page, make sure they follow it. If you're talking about Pinterest, show them what you've been doing with it. This is great promotion for the library and gives your patron a good example of one use of the technology.

DEALING WITH DIFFICULTIES

Since public librarians deal mostly with adults, there generally aren't many problems with students, behavior wise. However, since we do deal with the public, there are occasionally some minor issues, like people talking during class. Different teachers deal with problems like these in different ways. Here are a few difficult situations you might run into.

Talking

You want patrons to engage as much as possible during classes. Sometimes people meet up with their friends before class. On several occasions, I've had patrons talk to each other through the entire class. Whenever possible, I ignore this. We want to create an environment where people feel comfortable asking questions and learning, and calling someone out creates the opposite of that. If the talking is really disruptive and has nothing to do with class, I might ask them if it's okay for us to move on. It almost never comes to this, though. If worse comes to worst, you could ask them to leave for the day.

Interruptions

I usually encourage people to stop me if they have a question, so interruptions don't really bother me. If you'd prefer to go through all of your material before you take questions, that's good information to share at the beginning of class.

Naysayers

I've taught a number of different types of classes over the years, and this is something that seems to come up most in Internet and social media classes. This type of patron comes to class but refuses to create an account or follow along. On a number of occasions, I've had patrons aggressively ask why anyone would want to do this, and in general be disparaging. This is a really hard situation to find yourself in. Remember that you can't change that person's mind. All you can really do is mitigate the damage with the rest of your students. So when someone tells you that something is stupid, try to respond with something to diffuse the situation. For example, you might give some version of "This isn't for everyone. It's okay if it's not for you. It's great that you came to learn about it anyway." Then move right on, hopefully before the person can engage you further. You may have to repeat some version of this several times. Don't feel bad—this doesn't reflect on you as a teacher.

Disparate Skill Sets

This scenario happens fairly often. You'll have a group of students who have a passing understanding of a particular service, along with one or two students that have difficulty with basic computer skills, including using a mouse, typing, or accessing the Internet. In this case, you really have to go with the skill level of most of the students. I try to spend maybe five minutes getting the rest up to speed, but it's often not enough. If that's the case, you should probably encourage those that are behind to come in for one-on-one help (or to attend a computer basics class, if your library offers one), and just watch for the rest of this class. Make sure you follow this up with your card and perhaps a phone call; you don't want these people to feel left behind. I've done this with several students over the years, with good success.

ABOUT THIS BOOK

This book provides you with the basics of how to teach patrons about a small sampling of social media sites. It covers how to prepare for each class, what to expect, issues you might encounter, and much more. You can use the content as a rough script to use when teaching, or as a basic outline to follow or adapt as you like. Feel free to use these however you wish. You might like to combine two or more to create a targeted class. Or you might prefer to use a handout in its entirety. Still other teachers might like to shorten some sections and embellish others. You should do whatever works for you and your audience. The idea here is to save you as much time and effort as possible.

Don't feel the need to read this book cover to cover, although you can certainly do so if you wish. Instead, just use the chapters that you are interested in teaching.

Finally, please be aware that social media is constantly changing and evolving. Despite our best efforts, there will probably be some changes to the sites mentioned between the time of publishing and purchase of this book. Be sure to take a few moments to go over the material and note any changes. It's a good idea to do this before each class even when you've written the content yourself.

CHAPTER 1

Twitter

Twitter is a fun, easy-to-use website, and a great place to start teaching. When Twitter came on the scene in 2006, many people regarded it as a new, abbreviated form of Facebook. As it has grown up, it's morphed into something much more interesting. Twitter these days is an awesome place to follow the news, keep up with professional development, get your daily dose of celebrity gossip, and lots more. The genius of Twitter is its brevity. It cut down the incredible amount of verbiage that was popular at the time of its creation (mostly due to the explosion of blogs) and provided concise, tailored information in easy-to-digest snippets. Twitter can easily fit into the daily life of just about anyone. If you have 10 minutes, you have plenty of time to catch up on what's going on in the world!

HOW TO PREPARE

So how do you get ready to teach a Twitter class? The first and best thing you can do is to use it yourself. It's hard to be confident about teaching something that you don't know inside and out. Your first step should be to create an account (or dust off your old one if you haven't used it in a while) and start using it. Play around with all the different features. Do some posting and searching. Follow a bunch of new people, and practice learning how to search better. Find a friend and send some DMs (Direct Messages). The more you use it, the better you'll feel. As you play, keep track of some of the things that made you anxious, and some of the things you had questions about. When you're figuring out your curriculum later, you'll be so glad you took the time to do this.

So what is Twitter? It's truly the original form of micro blogging. Posts can include links and mentions and just about anything else you'd like, but they must be under 140 characters. That number includes spaces and punctuation, so brevity is key. Twitter works on a system of following. If I like something you have to say, I'll follow you and will automatically see anything you post on my home page. You can follow me back, or choose not to. Unlike Facebook, Twitter doesn't require a relationship to be reciprocal for it to exist. I follow many people on Twitter who do not follow me back, and vice versa.

COMMON QUESTIONS AND CONCERNS

Why Twitter?

The most common question that pops up in a Twitter class is, "Why would anyone want to do this?" It's a tough question, and it can set the tone for the entire class, since it's inevitably the first thing you'll be asked. The first few times I taught the class, I really struggled with the answer. Over the years, I have found that the best way to answer this question is with another. Ask your patron what they like to do, or what is really important to them. If they really love gardening, use the search function to show them the thousands of people—many of whom they know already—who post about it. The same with technology, cooking, parenting, networking, or anything else in the world. The best way to sell a technology like this is to show your patrons how useful it can be in their own lives. Twitter is an incredibly helpful tool, and really sells itself once people understand how it can be used. Approaching the question in this way helps to frame Twitter as something they're doing not because they have to (kids are nagging them to, their boss wants them to use it at work, etc.), but because it's useful and interesting.

Reluctance to Create an Account

In almost every social media class I teach, there is inevitably someone who doesn't want to make an account. That person will pretty much always tell you that they're just there to watch and learn what it's all about. This is perfectly fine, and I usually deal with it by letting the person know that if they change their mind, they can come to me for a one-on-one session on how to sign up. Then I'll take a moment to show the class how to search Google for a Twitter account they are interested in. Twitter no longer has a search feature on their front page, but you can easily search Google for "Better Homes and Gardens Twitter" and see that account with all of its tweets. People really like this cheat, since it's a great way to engage with Twitter and get something out of it without committing to it.

Privacy and Security Concerns

Often patrons may express concern about security in this class. This always seems odd to me, since Twitter asks for the least amount of personal information of just about any social network, but your patron doesn't know that. It's good to stress this with them. I always recommend that these patrons use an email set up for junk mail to sign up, and to keep their username generic. They don't need a profile picture, and Twitter doesn't ask for much of anything except an email address. It's incredibly easy to be anonymous on Twitter! Indeed, this is a great time to mention that they don't need to post on Twitter—many people never do—they can just use it and follow other people.

POSSIBLE CLASS VARIATIONS

Twitter for Business

There are lots of possible class variations for Twitter, but the one I've seen most is Twitter for business. This is essentially your basic Twitter class, with some information on marketing thrown in. This can be difficult for us to teach since most of us don't have a business background, but a bit of research will serve you well. Lots of sites have great resources for this, and it's helpful to include those links on any handouts you provide.

When I've taught Business Twitter in the past, I've stressed a few things that I thought were most important. The first is the 80/20 rule, although this number seems to change every time I see it. The basic principle is that 80 percent of the content you post should be interesting, while the other 20 percent can be promotional. The interesting content that your students choose can and should have something to do with their type of business, but shouldn't directly promote it. So if your patron is a real estate agent, they could post articles on how to stage a home, posts on buying trends, and maybe a few funny or offbeat houses they've found online. The other 20 percent can be promotional—links to open houses, invitations to events, etc. The idea here is to keep the casual reader who may not immediately need the services of the business engaged with their content. Once they do need those services, they'll hopefully be reminded of the business that they've been following.

The second thing to suggest is that it's okay for them to cheat a little when they're starting out. Suggest that your patrons study the Twitter pages of competing companies to see what they're doing that your patrons like and don't like. What tweets are people really responding to? Is their mix of content working? What are they doing really well, and what isn't working for them? Business owners can benefit greatly from looking at the frequently circulated lists of top business Twitter accounts. Most of those companies have people that are being paid to generate content. By emulating those accounts, your business owner can get ahead a little easier.

The third very valuable thing to mention is that businesses can do some really terrific networking via Twitter. They can follow similar businesses, vendors they'd like to work with, and potential clients, as well as the general public. Twitter often serves as a great equalizer. It's possible that the owner of a small computer business in a tiny town could speak with and cultivate a relationship with huge tech icons on Twitter. It happens every day, and can happen for your patrons, too.

Finally, it's important to emphasize that responsiveness is absolutely key on social networking, especially on Twitter. Businesses should be checking their Twitter pages just as frequently as they check their email. If someone airs a complaint about a business, the person responsible for the page should contact him or her immediately (and not over a DM) and attempt to fix the problem. It's vital that those who see the initial complaint also see the helpful response, so keep it all public. Many business owners aren't even on Twitter, because they worry about this happening; but it's truly a blessing in disguise. Everyone understands that sometimes mistakes happen—it's great to point out that it is their response that sets them apart from their competitors.

INSTRUCTOR NOTES

Logistics

I generally teach Twitter as a 60- to 90-minute class with extra time for questions afterward. The amount of time you take will depend on how much you cover, how quickly your patrons catch on, and how much time you give for practice.

What Is Twitter?

- Twitter is a website that connects friends and strangers through the use of "micro blogging"—messages shorter than 140 characters.
- Twitter allows people to share these "tweets" by answering the question, "What are you doing?"

How Twitter Can Be Used

- Twitter has become popular in the last few years as a way to quickly and easily keep people up to date on each other's lives. It can also be used for marketing and for gauging public opinion on popular topics. News organizations and celebrities are some of the most followed.
- Twitter has also become an important tool for tracking breaking news. For example, a few years ago when a plane crashed into the Hudson River, Twitter broke the story first, with big news networks following soon after. This has become increasingly common as more people use social media on their phones.

- In this class, we'll
  - Set up Twitter accounts
  - Learn how to search for topics and users, and
  - Post our first tweets

How Do I Create an Account?

- Start by going to www.twitter.com. On the right side of the screen, you should see a sign-in box on top with a signup option below. Fill out the form, including your name, your email address, and the password you would like to use to sign in. Make a note of this information, as you will need it each time you sign in to your account.
- Click the orange button that says **Sign up for Twitter.**
- You'll see a page with a brief form.
- Review this form. Uncheck the **Keep me signed on this computer** and **Tailor Twitter based on my recent website visits** boxes.
- If everything else looks okay, click **Create my account.**
- A short tutorial will appear to introduce you to common Twitter functions. Follow the prompts to go through the tutorial. These will require you to add five people to follow on Twitter. This is easy! A directory of the most followed people (mostly celebrities) will appear on the left side of the screen.
- Click **Follow** on five of these. The next two screens ask for basic info about you. Feel free to click **Skip.** Don't worry—everything you're doing right now can be changed later. Your screen should now have a skinny bar on the left side (mostly containing suggestions for new people to follow and a search bar) and a main reading pane on the left.
- Twitter will send a confirmation email to the address you signed up with. Open your email and click the blue box that says **Confirm your account now.** That's it! The page you're currently looking at will be the one you see each time you sign into Twitter.

USING TWITTER
Starting Out

- The layout of your Twitter page is pretty simple. Let's start with the top left corner and work our way around the page. The box in the upper left-hand corner includes your account information. You'll see your name, the number of tweets you've posted, the number of people you follow, and the number of people who follow you.
- Click on your name anytime to get to your profile page. That page has lots of great content for you and is the perfect place for you to go to find everything you need in one place.

- As you can see, your profile page provides suggestions on people you might like to follow, displays real-time Twitter trends, and gives you lots of options for editing your information and adding a profile picture. Feel free to do as much or as little with this page as you'd like. A great place to get started is the **Edit profile** button on the right side of the page.

How to Tweet

- Next, let's take a look at how to actually tweet, or post with Twitter. If you're in the profile page, you'll need to click the **Home** button to get to your main Twitter page again. Below the follower/ following information (again, in the upper left-hand corner), you'll see an empty white box.
- Click in this box to type in your tweet. Keep an eye on the character count next to the **Tweet** button. Once you reach 140 characters (letters and spaces both count), you won't be able to type any more—so keep it short and sweet!
- You'll also see a camera icon and a pin in this box. Clicking the camera opens up a directory of your computer so that you can upload a picture. The pin icon lets you check in, or add a location to your posting.
- When you've finished composing your message, click **Tweet**, and what you've written will show up in the feeds of those who follow you.

Posting Videos

- Love videos? Check out Vine, a way to post a six-second video to your Twitter page right from your phone.
- To use Vine, just go to the website at vine.co, or download the app in your app store.

Following Others

- On the right side of the page, you'll see another box labeled **Who to follow**. Twitter automatically generates these suggestions based on who you already follow. You'll also see promoted accounts here, meaning that the company who owns them pays to appear in the suggested lists for many accounts. Click **Refresh** or **View all** to see more suggestions.
- To follow someone, just click the blue-and-white **Follow** button below their name. It's good to remember that you don't need to know someone to follow them on Twitter.
- **Find people you know** uses your address book to find your contacts.

Following Trends

- Now look for a box called **Trends,** located below the box you composed a tweet in. These are generally current events and people that are being mentioned most on Twitter at the moment. Notice that all of these are hyperlinked. Clicking on any of them searches Twitter for all tweets that mention that word or phrase. You'll also notice that some of them begin with hashtags (e.g., #chocolate). Many people use hashtags (which look like this: #) to make phrases more searchable. Lots of people use these as searching tools to keep up with current events and news. They're also helpful for conferences and big meetings, since they gather notes from many people into one place.

Responding and Sharing

- Next, let's look at the pane in the middle of the screen. Under the headline **Tweets,** you'll see the most recent messages by people that you follow. Here people share articles, pictures, and ideas. Move your mouse over any of them and you'll see a number of options appear.
- **Reply** responds to the original poster. Clicking this link will open a box with the Twitter name of that person after the @ symbol. Type in your message and hit **Tweet.** Remember that this is public.
- **Retweet** allows you to repost the content without changing anything. Once you've retweeted something, your followers will see it.
- **Favorite** will mark the post with a gold star. You'll be able to go back and view the things you've marked easily. Change your mind? You can click **Unfavorite** to remove the item from your favorites list.
- The . . . **More** button takes you to a page that lets you embed a tweet into a website. You probably won't ever need this feature, but it's nice to know about.

Bells and Whistles

- If the tweet contains a link, you'll see something below it that says **View Summary.** This will show you the first few lines of the article. To read more, just click the original link. If you don't want to read the article, either skip it or click **Hide Summary.**
- You might also see a link that says **Expand.** Clicking that will show you comments from other Twitter users.
- Below the tweet itself, you'll see some brief stats about it. This will tell you who has retweeted and "favorited" it.
- If a tweet is offensive to you or contains spam, you have two options. First, you can unfollow the tweeter. If you'd prefer not to

do that, you can always click the **Flag Media** and the Twitter team will review the post.

- Want to see more by a particular person? Just click their name in your Twitter feed. You'll see a profile page that includes their statistics, a handful of their most recent tweets, and a blue button that says **Following**. If you'd rather not follow that person any more, just click the **Following** button and their content will no longer appear in your feed. This isn't permanent—you can always follow them again if you'd like.
- Want to see more? Click **Go to full profile** at the bottom of the page.

Using the Navigation Bar

- Now take a look at the bar at the top of the page. This contains some basic site navigation and searching features.
- The **Home** button always takes you back to your main Twitter page. It's the option at the top of the page on the far left side. Just look for the house icon.
- Click **Notifications** to see recent interactions with you and your content.
- **#Discover** is dedicated to giving you more people to follow. On this page you'll see a tailored list of people Twitter thinks you might like as well as a selection of tweets that you might find interesting. If you like the tweet, you can click on the name of the poster to see more content and follow them. At this point Twitter doesn't know much about you, so your suggestions will mainly be very popular accounts. As you follow more people, Twitter will provide better suggestions based on your interests.
- **Me** will take you to your profile page.

Searching

- The gray box with the magnifying glass to the right of the center lets you search for people or things. Click in the box and type your terms. As you type, a list of possible matches will appear. You'll notice right away that search terms appear first, then Twitter accounts. Click on one of those if it matches your search; otherwise, keep typing. You can hit Enter or click the magnifying glass to get your results.
- Next to the search box, you'll see an envelope for **Direct messages**. Click on this to write someone a private message. In the popup box that appears, just click **New message**. An empty box will appear.
- As you begin to type the name of the Twitter user in this box, a drop-down box will appear listing possible matches. Select the person you

wish to "talk to" from this menu. Once you've done this, you can type your message in the box below. Remember that this can only be 140 characters, too, so keep it short!

- When you're done typing, click the **Send message** box in the lower right-hand corner of the popup screen. The person you've messaged will see your message and their reply will appear in the same place.

Organizing, Shortcuts, Settings, and Signing Out

- Next to the Direct messages envelope, you'll see a gear icon. Click this to access many account features. The first option, **Edit profile**, is a shortcut to your profile page where you can update your information. Next is **Lists**. These are made up of groups of people that you create. So, for example, you could create a family list that shows only the tweets of those you are related to. Many people use this feature to organize their Twitter accounts a little better.
- The next item in the drop-down is a link to the **Help**. This is a great resource to check out if you have a question or want to learn more about something.
- **Keyboard shortcuts** does exactly what it says. It will display a list of keyboard combinations that will make using Twitter faster for you.
- **Settings** comes next in the menu. This page gives you lots of options. You can change your password, adjust the look of your Twitter page, set up email notifications, and much more.
- If you ultimately decide that Twitter isn't quite right for you, you can remove your account by clicking **Deactivate my account** at the bottom of the main **Settings** page. If you have second thoughts, you can reactivate your account within 30 days.
- Back in our drop-down menu under the gear, the last option is **Sign out**. If you have a shared computer, you should always log out when you're finished with Twitter for the day. This will prevent someone from inadvertently or deliberately tweeting from your account.
- The final icon in our navigation bar is a blue box with a feather. This, like the rest of the navigation bar, is visible on every page. It is a fast and easy shortcut to compose a new tweet.

Closing

That's it! Now you know how to use Twitter like a pro. If you have questions, please feel free to come in anytime for one-on-one help. Below, please find our list of most popular, fun, and handy Twitter accounts. These should help you get started. Happy tweeting!

TWITTER ESSENTIALS

What Is Twitter?

- Twitter is a website that connects friends and strangers through the use of "micro blogging"—messages shorter than 140 characters.

How Do I Create an Account?

- Start by going to www.twitter.com. On the right side of the screen you should see a sign-in box on top with a signup option below. Fill out the form, including your name, your email address, and the password you would like to use to sign in. Make a note of this information, as you will need it each time you sign in to your account.

How to Tweet

- On your **Home** page, look for an empty white box on the left side of the screen.
- Click in this box to type in your tweet. You'll have 140 characters—including spaces!
- The camera and pin icons also located in this box let you upload photos and add a location to your post.
- When you've finished composing your message, click **Tweet**.
- Want to post a video? Try Vine!

How to Follow Others

- On the right side of the page, you'll see another box that says **Who to follow**. Twitter makes these suggestions based on who you already follow. Click **Refresh** or **View all** to see more suggestions.
- To search for someone, use the gray box with the magnifying glass on the top of the page. To follow them, just click their name, then the blue-and-white **Follow** button below their name on the profile page that appears.
- **Find people you know** uses your address book to look for people that you know.

Following Trends

- **Trends** are generally current events and people that are being mentioned the most on Twitter at the moment. You'll see that all of these are hyperlinked. Clicking on any of them will search Twitter for all tweets that mention that word or phrase. Many people use hashtags (which look like this: #) to make these phrases more searchable.

Responding and Sharing

- Find the pane in the middle of your home screen. Under the headline **Tweets**, you'll see the most recent messages by people that you follow. Move your mouse over any of them and you'll see a number of options.

From *Teaching Social Media: The Can-Do Guide* by Liz Kirchhoff.
Santa Barbara, CA: Libraries Unlimited. Copyright © 2014.

- **Reply** responds to the original poster. Clicking this link will open a box with the Twitter name of that person after the @ symbol. Type in your message and hit **Tweet**. Remember that this is public.
- **Retweet** allows you to repost the content without changing anything. Once you've retweeted something, your followers will see it.

Account Information

- **Me** will take you to your profile page.
- **Settings** will give you lots of options. You can change your password, the look of your Twitter page, set up email notifications, and much more.
- **Deactivate my account** is located at the bottom of the **Settings** page.
- Back in our drop-down menu under the gear, the last option is **Sign out**. If you have a shared computer, you should always log out when you're finished with Twitter for the day.

Privacy

- The first step to privacy online is always to monitor what you're sharing in the first place.
- To access the privacy and security settings, click the gear in the upper right-hand corner of each page, then select **Settings**. Here you can change your password, protect your account, and much more.

URL Shorteners

- **TinyURL:** www.tinyurl.com
- **Bitly:** www.bitly.com
- **Ow.ly:** http://ow.ly/url/shorten-url

Terms

- **Tweet:** A short, 140-character message that shares an idea, a website, a picture, and more.
- **Following:** The Twitter users that you follow.
- **Followers:** Twitter users that follow you.
- **Hashtag (#):** This symbol helps to denote keywords and phrases and can make them more easily searchable.
- **@:** Starts a username, often used to tag a person.
- **Trends:** What Twitter users are talking about the most right now.
- **Retweet (RT):** Shares a tweet from someone else without changing it.
- **Modified tweet (MT):** Shares a tweet that you have changed.
- **Direct message (DM):** A private message between you and someone else.
- **Vine:** Six seconds of video that you can upload with your phone. To use it, download the app from your app store.

Tips for Finding More Users to Follow

- Google "top twitter (year)" to get access to the many lists of the most popular and interesting Twitter accounts of the year.

(continued)

From *Teaching Social Media: The Can-Do Guide* by Liz Kirchhoff.
Santa Barbara, CA: Libraries Unlimited. Copyright © 2014.

- Use the Twitter search feature to look for a keyword or topic that interests you.
- Look at the followers and following lists of those you follow.

Resources

- **Mashable Twitter guide:** http://mashable.com/category/twitter/
- **Twitter on Twitter:** https://twitter.com/twitter
- **Twitter Help Center:** https://support.twitter.com/groups/50-welcome-to-twitter#

Instructors: the following section is great to include with your handout. You can link to these accounts if you post your handouts online! It's a nice touch to include a few local businesses or important people on this list too. It's easy to find the username. Just use the search box to find the person you're looking for. The username is listed right next to the real name of the account holder.

TWITTER ACCOUNTS YOU MAY WANT TO FOLLOW

News

BBC Breaking News: @BBCBreaking
Breaking News: @BreakingNews
CNN Breaking News: @cnnbrk
Fox News: @FoxNews
New York Times: @nytimes
NPR News: @nprnews
Reuters Live: @ReutersStream
Time Magazine: @TIME
TWC Breaking: @TWCBreaking

Tech

Arstechnica: @arstechnica
Engadget: @engadget
Mashable: @mashable
New York Times Tech: @nytimestech
Tech Crunch: @TechCrunch
Wired: @wired

Science

Brian Cox: @ProfBrianCox
Richard Dawkins: @RichardDawkins
Discovery Channel: @Discovery

Culture

Lyric Opera: @LyricOpera
Museum Nerd: @museumnerd
New York Public Library: @nypl

Fashion

Tyra Banks: @tyrabanks
Michael Kors: @MichaelKors
Kate Upton: @KateUpton

(continued)

From *Teaching Social Media: The Can-Do Guide* by Liz Kirchhoff.
Santa Barbara, CA: Libraries Unlimited. Copyright © 2014.

Food

Barefoot Contessa: @inagarten
Anthony Bourdain: @Bourdain
Foodmentary: @foodmentary
Smitten Kitchen: @smittenkitchen
Saveur Magazine: @saveurmag

Parenting

Honest Toddler: @HonestToddler
Parenting.com: @parenting

Authors

Margaret Atwood: @MargaretAtwood
Harlan Coben: @HarlanCoben
Sarah Dessen: @sarahdessen
Neil Gaiman: @neilhimself
George RR Martin: @GeorgeRRMartin
Brad Meltzer: @bradmeltzer
Joyce Carol Oates: @JoyceCarolOates
Chuck Palahniuk: @chuckpalahniuk
Jodi Picoult: @jodipicoult
JK Rowling: @jk_rowling
Nicholas Sparks: @NicholasSparks

CHAPTER 2

Foursquare

In the past few years, the use of location services has exploded in social networking. As the first of these services, Foursquare deserves a bit of attention. In this chapter, you'll find out how to include Foursquare in your classes. The service itself doesn't generally have enough substance to it for an entire class, but it can easily be combined with other social media sites for a great, well-rounded class.

When Foursquare started in 2009, it was mostly meant to act as a way for friends to connect. When your friend checked in at the coffee shop near you, you got a notification and could head over to say "hi." As you might imagine, this was especially great for college students. As the service has evolved, it's become a robust city guide and recommendation service. Its power lies in the ability to share personal tips and recommendations for an incredible variety of places. The fact that it has been able to adapt in this way probably accounts for its survival. Tons of websites now have check-ins as part of their services, so if that's all Foursquare ever did, it would probably have shut down by now.

HOW TO PREPARE

Because Foursquare is used primarily with the GPS on a cell phone, you'll need to take this into consideration when you're preparing to teach. You can take screenshots and embed them in a PowerPoint, but it may be easier for you to use your own phone to do a live demo in class. At my library, I use an adapter to connect my phone to the projector on our AV system, but your setup may be different. Just be sure to practice with the technology first—you want to avoid any nasty surprises!

Since I teach Foursquare in conjunction with a number of other services and my patrons aren't usually that interested in checking in themselves, I generally don't go into how to create an account beyond showing people where to click to sign up. I spend most of the time focusing on searching Foursquare for useful content. It's also helpful to mention that the app is the cornerstone of the service. I always show students what the app icon looks like so that they know what to look for in their app store. If you have time, it would be helpful to do a quick app overview.

COMMON QUESTIONS AND CONCERNS

Lots of people are especially concerned about the idea of checking in somewhere. Obviously, you aren't home when you check in at the coffee shop, so many people worry about break-ins and that type of thing. Over the life of the service, this hasn't been as much of an issue as many people initially feared, which does help reassure students.

I've taught Foursquare as part of a number of classes and frequently find that folks who are there generally just want to learn about it. They often aren't interested in making an account or using the service; they just want to know what it's about and how it's used. This is totally fine! If your patron decides they'd like to create an account, they'll come to you for help later.

POSSIBLE CLASS VARIATIONS

I've taught Foursquare most frequently as part of travel classes. It's a great discovery tool when you aren't sure what's good in the area you are in. The class I teach most often is called "Plan Your Trip Online," and it uses Foursquare, Yelp, RoadTrip America, Expedia, Hotwire, TripAdvisor, Travelzoo, and lots of other services to help people save time and money when planning their next vacation.

I've also used Foursquare in another class on couponing online. This uses lots of websites and apps to clip coupons and find deals. Foursquare has lots of check-in deals, so this is a perfect place for it!

You might find that lots of business owners come to this class. Foursquare is a great place to offer customers deals and add-on services, so it's a good service for a business owner to know about. If you'd like to, you could also include this service in a class on marketing.

INSTRUCTOR NOTES

Logistics

As previously mentioned, the content below can be used as part of a class covering a number of different social media websites. I generally expect the portion focusing on Foursquare to take between 15 and 20 minutes.

What is Foursquare?

- Foursquare is a simple, easy-to-use website and mobile app that allows you to "check in" or tell your friends and followers where you are.
- Although it started as simply a way to connect people, Foursquare now uses community-suggested tips as a way to create a really robust and excellent city and location guide.
- Lots of businesses now use Foursquare as a way to offer deals and coupons just for checking in at their location. It's a great way to save some money or get a little something special!

How Do I Create an Account?

- Creating an account is easy and free! Just go to www.four square.com. In the top right-hand corner of the page, there are two boxes. Click the one that says **Sign Up**. You'll have the option to sign up with Facebook, Google+, or your email. Click your preferred method.
- Next, you'll see a page with a short form to fill out. Be sure to make a note of your username and password. Please note that you only need to provide the information that is marked with an asterisk (*).
- When you're finished filling in the form, click the giant green button at the bottom that says **Sign Up**.
- Once you submit your information, you'll see a page with several different phones on it. To use Foursquare to check in, you'll need a smartphone (or a phone with Internet) and the free Foursquare app. You can click on the box below your phone to get the app, or just find it in your app store. You do not need the app or a smartphone to search Foursquare for information about a location. Feel free to skip this step by clicking **Find Your Friends**.
- The next page will ask you to find your friends by clicking the appropriate icon. Currently you can use Facebook, Twitter, or email to find people. If you choose Facebook or Twitter, a popup will ask you to authorize Foursquare to see and use information from these services. Once you authorize it, Foursquare will show you a list of

friends that also use Foursquare. Add the ones you'd like, then click **Okay, I'm Done Adding Friends.**

- After you click this, you'll see your main account page. Here you'll find lots of ways to find new places to try, new friends, and more. Because Foursquare really wants you to use their service on the app, you'll also see lots of links to the various app stores.

How Do I Use Foursquare?

- If you're interested in using Foursquare to check in and let your friends know where you are, it's easy. Find the Foursquare app in your app store on your phone, and download it.
- Open the app by touching it. A popup will appear asking if you'd like Foursquare to use your current location. Allow it to do so.
- Now click **Log In** and fill in the requested information.
- Once you reach the main account screen, you'll see a yellow **Check In** button. Touch that and Foursquare will give you a list of nearby locations to check in. Just touch the one you're at.
- If you use Facebook, the next page will be very familiar. Foursquare will give you a place to write a note about what you're doing or where you're at. You can click **I'm with . . .** to tag people (indicating that you were there with them) or use the **Photo** button to add your photo of the place. When you've put in all the info you want to, just touch **Check In Here.**
- It's great to check in when you get to a place! When you finish checking in, you'll see tips from other users—super handy if you're trying a new restaurant or service.
- Lots of Foursquare listings include the business phone number, website, and even menu information if available. This can be really helpful to have!
- That's all there is to checking in! Once you've checked in once, you'll start receiving badges. These are little pieces of "flair" you get for checking in at particular places (say, five Chinese restaurants) or a particular number of times. For example, the first time you check in, you'll get the Newbie badge. Lots of people love this game-like aspect of Foursquare, but it's actually very useful to those who don't even check in. When you go to a restaurant and see that the mayor (the person who has been there the most times) has recommended a particular dish, it's an indication that someone who really knows the place thinks it's one of the best things to have.

Searching

- In this class, we're primarily focusing on how to use Foursquare to find information or deals on a particular location, so let's talk about searching.
- Searching can be done either on your computer or in the app. The two are very similar. The search box on the website is on the top of the screen. Look for a long white box that says **I'm Looking For** ... with another next to it with your location. On the app, this is the white box on the top of the screen that says **Browse Nearby**. Just type the search term in either to find what you're looking for.
- Let's start searching. Say you're looking for restaurants near your location. Just type in "restaurant" or the type of food you're in the mood for. So if I tell Foursquare I'm hungry for Chinese and I'm in Chicago, Illinois, I'll come up with a list of nearby restaurants. In a place like Chicago, that'll be a lot, and many of them won't be very close. To get better results, click the arrow that appears in the box that lists your city. This will show restaurants that are closest to you first, and will save you a lot of time.
- Now that you've got your list of possible restaurants, it's time to see what people say. Click on a listing to see more about it. For example, if I were to click on the Peking Mandarin Restaurant in Irving Park, I'd see that other Foursquare users recommend the spicy seafood soup, that people recommend the wings, and lots more. If you decide you aren't interested in the Peking Mandarin Restaurant, you can always use the back button on your browser to return to your search page so you can keep browsing.
- That's really all there is to browsing and finding information on Foursquare! Take a few moments and practice now.

Closing

As you can see, Foursquare is a quick and easy website and app with tons of handy information. Use it with other services like Yelp to save yourself tons of time, bad meals, and maybe even some money!

FOURSQUARE ESSENTIALS

What It Is

- Foursquare is a simple, easy-to-use website and mobile app that allows you to "check in" or tell your friends and followers where you are. It's also a great way to find out about a city or location and connect with area businesses for coupons and promotions.

How to Sign Up

- Creating an account is easy and free! Just go to www.foursquare.com and follow the prompts.

How to Check In

- To use Foursquare to check in, you'll need a smartphone (or a phone with Internet) and the free Foursquare app. If you don't want to check in, you can use the website or app to search.
- If you're interested in using Foursquare to check in and let your friends know where you are, it's easy. Find the Foursquare app in your app store on your phone and download it.
- Follow the prompts to turn on location services and log in.
- Touch the yellow **Check In** button and Foursquare will prompt you to select from a list of nearby locations to check in at. Add any information you'd like and touch **Check In Here**.

How to Search

- Searching can be done either at the top of the screen on your computer or in the app on your mobile device. The two processes are very similar. Just type the search term in either to find what you're looking for.
- Start searching. To get better results, click the arrow to see locations nearest to you first.

Terms

- **Check In:** Tells your friends and followers where you are, and can make you eligible for specials and deals.
- **Badges:** Flair for milestones—for example, for a certain number of check-ins.
- **Mayors:** The Foursquare user that has checked in the most times at a location.

Resources

- **Mashable Foursquare Guide:** http://mashable.com/category/foursquare/
- **Foursquare User Guide:** http://support.foursquare.com/home

From *Teaching Social Media: The Can-Do Guide* by Liz Kirchhoff.
Santa Barbara, CA: Libraries Unlimited. Copyright © 2014.

CHAPTER 3

Yelp

Yelp is one of the handiest websites out there, and a snap to teach. It's a highly useful consumer review website that can help you find information about a variety of businesses and services in your area. These reviews are helpful not just for obvious uses ("How is the restaurant down the street?"), but also for finding information on bus lines, management companies, and nearly anything else you can think of. As one of the oldest review sites around, Yelp is an extremely rich and helpful resource with millions of reviews.

HOW TO PREPARE

Preparing for your class should be fairly simple and straightforward. Yelp is a location-specific service, so before class begins, identify a number of examples of businesses in your area to demonstrate to your students. I usually prepare ahead of time by searching for a few restaurants, a salon, a store, and a few services (perhaps a local dog walker). While you're teaching, you can use these examples as places to search for reviews and targeted information. You might consider pairing Yelp with some other services you are teaching. Like Foursquare, it works great as part of travel and couponing classes. You could also consider bundling it with a number of other review sites like TripAdvisor. I generally teach Yelp as a demonstration class, since I like to pair it with other services, but do what works for you and your community.

COMMON QUESTIONS AND CONCERNS

Most people understand Yelp to some extent, and often your students will already be users; so you shouldn't run into many problems teaching this class. However, be prepared to discuss Yelp's controversial decision to filter reviews. This was done to prevent users from making accounts to promote a business (generally their own, or a friend's) or to flame or discredit a competitor. Filtered results can be seen by anyone (just click the phrase at the bottom of the business page that says something like **10 other reviews that are not currently recommended**) but they do not count as part of the overall stars a business receives.

Reviews can be filtered for any number of reasons. Frequently, a user will be filtered for their first several reviews. Once they've established a bit of a history, their reviews will appear again. The filtering process is completely automated, so users or reviews can't be manually reinstated by Yelp. Those who have their reviews blocked will generally see them reinstated after they post more reviews and fill out their profiles.

POSSIBLE CLASS VARIATIONS

Yelp works great as part of a number of classes. Try it with location-based services or review services. You can also teach it as part of a class on couponing, travel, apps, and lots more.

As you're preparing for your class, you might want to consider doing a short tutorial on the app. It has a great location service that recommends nearby businesses, as well as a nifty service called Monocle. Monocle uses the camera in a phone to display the locations (including their listing information) over the top of whatever the camera is pointing at. If you were standing on a corner and searching for a new restaurant, you'd be able to see the street in front of you with the "pins" for the restaurants where they're actually located. It's a little like a real-life map. I usually demonstrate this feature in class—patrons really like it!

INSTRUCTOR NOTES

Logistics

This is a service that can be covered either in a short class or a portion of a class including one or more other websites. Plan to take 20–30 minutes for your teaching time, with questions.

What Is Yelp?

- Yelp is an incredibly useful consumer review website that can help you find information about a variety of businesses and services in your area. Yelp provides information not only on restaurants where you are, but also local bus lines, shops, management companies, and nearly anything else in a particular location.
- It's free to use and easy to search by address, town, or zip code.

How Do I Use Yelp?

- It's easy! Open your favorite web browser and type in www.yelp.com.
- Not sure exactly what you're looking for? Use the **Best of Yelp** feature, located in the middle of the page on the left side. There are a few popular categories listed there—for example, **Restaurants** or **Shopping**. To see the list of businesses, click the category name. The middle of the page features a selection from each category to browse.
- Prefer to search? Just use the search box at the top of the page to put in what you want and the location. For example, search for **sushi** and **Chicago, IL**. In this particular search, you get more than 400 results. The search also works for specific companies.
- If you get too many results, use the filters on the top of the page to narrow your results by price, location, number of reviews, and other factors.
- Each business listing includes the name, type, starred rating, number of reviews, and contact information. Click the name of the restaurant to see reviews and additional information.
- To see filtered reviews, scroll to the bottom of the page of search results. On the left side of the page you'll see something that says **10 other reviews that are not currently recommended**. If you click on this phrase you'll be able to see the reviews that were not immediately available to you. You may have to type a CAPTCHA (meant to thwart spammers, this is a short code that is typed in by a user to access a page).

How Do You Evaluate Reviews?

- Remember that many people review a business only if they are very satisfied or very dissatisfied.
- When evaluating reviews, look for themes more than ratings. For example, if several people mention a particular problem with a business, you'll know to watch out for that issue when working with the company.
- Use the reviews to find a particularly good employee at a company. For example, many salon reviews mention the same few hairdressers over and over. It's an easy way to find out which ones are great, and which ones should be avoided.
- Reading negative reviews isn't necessarily a waste of your time. Many times, a negative review points to businesses and services that are better.

How Do I Create an Account?

- To add reviews to Yelp, you need to create an account. Fortunately, this only takes a few minutes.

- Start by clicking **Sign Up**, located in the upper right-hand corner of the page.
- Fill out the short form with your name, email address, password, and some brief demographic information. Click the **Sign Up** button at the bottom right-hand corner of the page.
- The next page asks if you'd like to find your Facebook friends on Yelp. Click **Skip this step** in the upper right hand corner to continue without providing this information.
- Next, you'll be asked to find friends via your email address book. Again, click **Skip this section**.
- Yelp will ask these two questions twice each. Feel free to continue skipping them.
- A confirmation email will be sent to the address you provided. Click on the link in the email to confirm your account and use the full features of the site. A window will then pop up confirming that your account has been set up. You may be asked to sign in. Close the window and your email and return to Yelp.
- The page you'll see once you've created an account gathers reviews and discussion on businesses near your location. Feel free to browse and see if anything is of interest to you.
- In the top right hand of your page, you should see your name in blue. If you click this link you'll be able to see your profile, the easiest place to add your information and pictures.

Writing Your First Review

- Now that you're all set up with an account and profile, you're ready to review. To start, click **Write a Review**, the third tab from the left side at the top of the page.
- Start by identifying the business and location. Click **Search Businesses**. A list of possible matches will appear. Click the **Write a Review** button next to the correct business. If you can't find the business, go ahead and add it with the **Add a Business** button at the bottom of the page.
- Now let's rate the business. Just mouse over the stars at the top of the page, and click to rate the establishment. Click in the review box and start typing your review. It can be as general or as specific as you'd like. When you're done, click **Post**.
- You're done! If you'd like to edit your review, you can do so in the **About Me** tab at the top of the page.

More Tools

- Use the Better Business Bureau to check out businesses ahead of time. Use the website at www.bbb.org or contact your area chapter.

- Use *Consumer Reports* to find quality, recommended products. Access *Consumer Reports* for free through most libraries.
- For services, check the *Consumers' Checkbook*.

Closing

Yelp is a helpful, easy to use website with a great app.

YELP ESSENTIALS

What It Is

- Yelp is an extremely useful consumer review website that can help you find information about a variety of businesses and services in your area. It's free and easy to use.

How to Search and Browse

- It's easy! Open your favorite web browser and type in www.yelp.com.
- To browse, try the **Best of Yelp** feature, which organizes businesses by category.
- Prefer to search? Just use the search box at the top of the page to put in what you want and the location. Use the provided filters to narrow your results by price, location, number of reviews, and more.
- If you'd like to see more reviews, look for those that have been filtered. To find these, scroll to the bottom of the page of search results. On the left side of the page you'll see something that says **10 other reviews that are not currently recommended**. If you click on the phrase, you'll be able to see the reviews that were not immediately available to you.

How to Evaluate Reviews

- Look for themes more than ratings. For example, if several people mention a particular problem with a business, you'll know to watch out for that issue when working with the company. This can also help you find the best employees and avoid the worst.
- Negative reviews often mention similar businesses to consider, so read carefully.

How to Create an Account

- Start by clicking **Sign Up**, located in the upper right-hand corner of the page.
- Fill out the short form and click the **Sign Up** button at the bottom right-hand corner of the page. Skip the steps that ask you to find friends.
- Confirm your account by checking your email and clicking the link provided.
- In the top right hand of your page, you should see your name in blue. If you click this link you'll be able to see your profile, the easiest place to add your information and pictures.

How to Write a Review

- To start, click **Write a Review**, the third tab from the left side at the top of the page.
- Start by identifying the business and location. Click **Search Businesses**. A list of possible matches will appear. Click the **Write a Review** button next to the correct business. If you can't find the business, go ahead and add it with the **Add a Business** button at the bottom of the page.

- Mouse over the stars at the top of the page and click to rate the establishment. Write your review in the provided box and click **Post**.
- To edit your review, click the **About Me** tab at the top of the page to access what you've written.

Resources
- **Mashable Yelp Guide:** http://mashable.com/category/yelp/
- **Yelp FAQ:** http://www.yelp.com/faq

From *Teaching Social Media: The Can-Do Guide* by Liz Kirchhoff.
Santa Barbara, CA: Libraries Unlimited. Copyright © 2014.

CHAPTER 4

Pinterest

Although it's a fairly new service, Pinterest has already established itself as one of the biggest social networks around. Back when it started, Pinterest was often maligned as being a silly time waster. More recently, Pinterest has emerged as a popular and powerful tool that has lots of benefits for both individuals and businesses.

The basic idea behind Pinterest is simple. Someone sees a pretty picture of something they'd like to save for later. They "pin" or save that picture to a themed board that helps them to organize their ideas and images. Pinterest grew quickly because it's beautiful and useful. It's easy to pull together images to help plan for a wedding, decorate a house, cook for your family, get into shape, and much more. Because it's so attractive and easy to use, people tend to spend way more time than they meant to while browsing it.

HOW TO PREPARE

Pinterest is such an easy class to teach and shouldn't require a great deal of preparation. The site and privacy settings are simple and straightforward, so most of the time you spend teaching will cover how to pin and how to find new sources of content. You may consider either skipping a handout or providing only a tips and tricks handout for this class.

COMMON QUESTIONS AND CONCERNS

It's good to be prepared for a few minor problems that you'll probably run into in your classes. Like Facebook, Pinterest can be extremely distracting. Your patrons will probably lose you, so prepare to repeat yourself frequently. Second, it's good to remind students that you can't control anything that they're about to see, and that they may find something offensive. This actually happens rarely, since Pinterest consists mostly of recipes and decorating and babies, but it's good to mention it. Finally, I do try to provide a caveat about copyright. Pinterest is basically a giant case of copyright infringement, so be sure to caution your patrons that if they are saving images for something really important (for example, a wedding), they might want to back up their information elsewhere. I'm inclined to think that if Pinterest was going to be shut down, it would have happened already, but it doesn't make sense to take chances.

POSSIBLE VARIATIONS

There are lots of possible variations for a Pinterest class. Pinterest for foodies is a fun one, as is Pinterest for wedding and party planning. It also works great to teach Pinterest in conjunction with Etsy, since businesses can create a store on Etsy, then pin their store items to Pinterest.

SPECIAL CONSIDERATIONS

Since Pinterest lends itself to fun class ideas, why not teach at a wine bar? Or maybe at an area business? This isn't a class that even needs much marketing, since almost everyone has heard of Pinterest and lots of people are eager to try it out.

Pinterest can generally be taught in one session of about an hour to an hour and a half. Leave lots of time for your patrons to play, and be prepared to repeat yourself often!

INSTRUCTOR NOTES

Logistics

Pinterest is a fast, easy class to teach. Plan for extra time though, since people do get distracted. Your class will probably take between 45 minutes and one hour.

What Is Pinterest?

- Pinterest is a fun, easy-to-use social bookmarking tool. Users "pin" or save beautiful, inspiring, or amazing images to "boards" or collections. Pins and boards are public, so it's easy to browse what other people love and find things that inspire you.
- Pinterest is fabulous for planning weddings and parties, redecorating the house, creating a collection of great recipes, designing a new

craft, and lots more. It's a great tool for saving images of anything that you might want to remember later.

- If you have pins or links that are especially important to you, you may want to back them up in a second location. Because Pinterest is a relatively new service, issues of copyright and fair use haven't been worked out yet. Although it's extremely unlikely, it is possible that the service could someday be shut down. So if you're planning your wedding, save your links somewhere else, too!
- In this class, we'll create a Pinterest account and learn how to pin, re-pin, organize, and much more.

How Do I Create an Account?

- It's easy! Start by going to www.pinterest.com.
- You'll see a few options on this first page. You can **Sign up with Facebook** or **Sign up with email**. Below these two options, you'll see something that says **Already have an account? Log in now**. You can use this bottom link to sign in from now on. Today, let's click **Sign up with email** to start. You can change this to sign in with your Facebook account later if you decide you'd prefer to do so.
- Create your account by providing the requested information. Be sure to write down your username and password combination, and keep it someplace where you can find it!
- Click the red button that says **Sign up**.
- Pinterest will now ask you to take a short tour. Take a moment to click through this—it gives you a brief overview of the site and how things work.
- As you click through, you'll find that the final prompt of this short tour asks you to choose five boards to follow. This is easy! On the left you'll see a list of categories like **Featured, Design**, and **DIY & Crafts**.
- It's not difficult to unfollow boards later, so pick a few from this list by first clicking on the category, then **Follow** below the board you like.
- Want more options? Click the **More Interests** button on the bottom of the left-hand side of the page.
- As you follow each board, a big red checkmark will appear where you previously saw the image of the board. Below that, you'll see a button that says **Unfollow**.
- If you look in the top right hand of the box you're working in, you'll see a series of checkboxes. These show you how many more boards to follow before you can go on. Finish adding your boards now.
- Done? Now click the red button that says **Try Out Your Feed**.

- Take a moment to open a new browser window and check your email. You'll need to do this to confirm your account with Pinterest. The email will contain a link for you to click on. This will launch a new Pinterest window with your account activated. You can close the old one now.
- Yay! You're set to go! You'll never have to do the previous part again. From now on, you'll simply click the log in link on the main page.

Using Pinterest

- Your Pinterest page is ready for you to use! Let's take a tour of your page. We'll start with the middle column, which is made up of the pins from the boards that you followed during the setup process. As you add more boards, the variety and number of pins will increase.
- Use the scroll bar on the right side of the page to view pins. You'll notice that the page refreshes frequently to bring you more content to see.
- Want to go back to the top of the page to see new things that have loaded? In the bottom right-hand corner of the screen you'll see an icon of an arrow pointing up with a horizontal line above it. Clicking this brings you to the top of your results.

Pinning

- See something you love? To save it for later, pin it! All you need to do is move your mouse over the image. Several options will appear.
- **Pin it** will save the picture for you. Go ahead and click this now.
- To pin something, you need to have a board (or a themed collection of pins) to pin to. Let's create one now. Just type in a name describing a group of things you'll want to pin. You can easily change the name later if you don't like it. When you're done typing, click **Create**. The name of the board will now be listed every time you want to pin something.
- Want to change the **Description** of the pin? Feel free to do so. Just click in the large box and type in your description or a reminder to yourself. This description can be helpful for decorating (i.e., "paint color for downstairs bathroom") or wedding planning. This box can't be left blank.
- When you're done, just click **Pin it**. The pin will be saved for you on the board you selected, and will be visible to those who follow you.
- Take a minute to practice pinning a few more items.

Other Options

- Now let's talk about sending images. Mouse over an image until you see the **Pin it** directory appear. This time you'll be looking for **Send**, located to the right of the pinning button we used just a moment ago. Click this to email or send directly to a friend. You can even include a message. Just type in the box that says **Add a message**.
- Finally, you can "favorite" an image. This doesn't save it to your boards. To do it, just click the heart icon on the upper right-hand corner of the image. When you click the icon, the heart turns red and the pin becomes accessible in **Your Likes**.

Finding the Source of a Pin

- Sometimes you'll want to find out more about a pin. To do this, just click the image. A new page will appear with information about the pin.
- You'll see the options to pin it and send it like before. On the right side of the page, Pinterest will show you the boards that the image came from. Below the picture, you'll see other boards that also contain the image. You can follow any of them right from this page.
- Keep scrolling down on the page to find pins that are similar to the original.
- On the top of the page next to the pin and like/unlike buttons, you'll see a button that says **Visit Site**. Click this to see where the pin came from.
- The visit site link is what makes Pinterest so useful for so much. Have a cooking board? Pin lots of great recipes! Clicking the website link will take you right to the webpage with the recipe. Planning a party or wedding? Create boards with your ideas for favors, decorations, and more. When you click any of the images, you'll be able to go right to the website they came from. There you'll find more information on where to buy or how to create the item.
- When you're done looking at this page, close it by clicking on the big "X" located in the upper right-hand corner of the page. This will take you back to your Pinterest home page.

Navigation and Searching

- Now let's explore the top navigation bar on your Pinterest page. On the far left side of your page, you'll see an icon made up of three dashes in a box. Click this to see a list of categories on Pinterest.
- Click on any category to see pins on that topic. If you want some great new recipes, click the **Food & Drink** category. Want to see the stuff that's being pinned the most? Just click **Popular**.

- Next to the categories icon, you'll see a search box. Type in a term here to see boards and pins on that topic. For example, if you'd like some chicken recipes, just type "chicken" in the box. The helpful drop-down menu will prompt you to click on "chicken recipes" or you can just hit Enter on your keyboard.
- If you look in the upper left-hand corner, you'll see that you can break down your results by clicking **Pins, Boards,** or **Pinners.** Searching for a topic is a great way to find new boards to follow.
- In the top middle of your navigation bar, you'll see the Pinterest logo. You can always click on this to get back to the home page you are familiar with.

Creating an Original Pin

- On the right side of the navigation bar, you should see an icon that looks like a plus sign. Click this to add a pin of your own. There are three options.
- The first, **Upload a pin,** allows you to choose an image file from your computer. This is a great option if you want to take and organize pictures of a renovation, a recent trip, a catalog of your recipes, and lots more. When pinners click through the original image to see the source, the original picture will appear without being linked to anything.
- The second option, **Add from a website,** lets you copy and paste a web address to pin an item. To do this, just click the URL bar (the one that you click in to type a web address) on the page you'd like to pin the picture from. It should turn blue. Left-click and choose **Copy.** Now go back to your Pinterest page, click the plus sign, and choose **Add from a website.** Pinterest will ask you where you'd like to pin from. Just click into the white box, then left-click your mouse. Select **Paste** and the URL you copied should appear. Click **Find images** to see all the pinnable content on the page. All the images from a page should appear with a **Pin it** button in the upper left-hand corner. Click it and add it to the board you'd like it to live on.
- Finally, **Recommended Pins** shows you pins that are similar to your own. Feel free to re-pin whatever you like!

Boards, Pins, and Account Settings

- Next to the plus-sign logo, you'll see a logo of a pin (your picture might be here if you've added one to your profile). This handy icon offers a drop-down menu that takes you to your boards, your pins, and other places on the site.

- **Your Profile & Pins** takes you to a page that shows you boards and stats. The top of the page has lots of handy information on how many boards you have, how many pins, and how many things you've liked. Below this, you'll see your boards. Each has an option to edit.
- Want to pin to a board with a friend or a group of people? You can give a board group privileges by clicking the edit button under it. Look for an option that says **Who can pin**. Type the name or email of the person you'd like to add and click **Invite**. Your board will become visible to that person and they'll be able to add content just like you do.
- Scroll down further, and you'll see something that says **Create a secret board**. Clicking this allows you to make a board that nobody can see but you. This is great for pinning ideas for surprise parties, baby items before you've announced, and anything else that you might not want to be public.
- **Find Friends** will show you boards from your friends on Facebook if you have chosen to sign in with that service.
- **Follow Boards** suggests interesting boards sorted by topic, or interest.
- **Visit Help Center** is a great place to go if you have a question or want to learn more. Pinterest publishes the most frequently asked questions, so you may be able to find the answer to your question immediately. If not, this is where you can go to contact the Pinterest team about any problems you're experiencing.
- **Settings** is the best place to go to change your password, clear your recent searches (this is a really nice feature to go with your private boards), manage the emails that Pinterest sends you, and more. Pinterest will also let you change how you sign in. If you prefer to sign in with Facebook or Twitter instead of your email, you can change those settings at the bottom of the page.
- Want to stop using Pinterest? Click **Deactivate** at the bottom of the **Settings** page.
- If you're on a shared computer, you should always use the **Log Out** option in the drop-down menu under the pin.
- Finally, in the far right corner of your screen, you'll see an icon with two pins or a number. This will show you notifications. This is a great place to see new followers as well as which of your pins are the most popular.

Closing

That's it! Now you know how to use Pinterest and can happily pin away. If you have questions, please feel free to come in anytime for one on one help.

PINTEREST ESSENTIALS

What Is Pinterest?

- Pinterest is a fun, easy-to-use social bookmarking tool. Users "pin" or save beautiful or inspiring images and websites to public or secret "boards" or collections.

How Do I Create an Account?

- It's easy! Start by going to www.pinterest.com.
- Click **Sign up with email** to start. You can sign in with your Facebook account later if you decide you'd prefer to do so.
- Create your account by providing the requested information and click **Sign up**. Take the short and easy Pinterest tour, and select a few boards to start following.
- Take a moment to check your email to confirm your account. Click the provided link to activate. Now you have an account and you're set to go!

How to Browse Pinterest

- Use the scroll bar on the right side of the page to view pins in the middle of the page. The page refreshes content to bring you more content to see.
- Click the upward arrow icon in the lower right hand of the page to bring you to the top of your results.

How to Pin

- See something you love? To save it for later, pin it! All you need to do is move your mouse over the image. Several options will appear.
- **Pin it** will save the picture for you. Go ahead and click this now.
- Now we'll need to create a board (or a themed collection of pins) to pin to. Type in a name describing a group of things you'll want to pin and click **Create**.
- Change the **Description** of the pin if you like, then click **Pin it**. The pin will be saved and will be visible to your followers.

Other Options

- To send a pin, mouse over it until you see the **Pin it** directory appear. Click **Send** to email or send directly to a friend.
- You can favorite an image by clicking the heart icon in the upper right-hand corner of the image. This doesn't save it to your boards, but does save it to **Your Likes**.

How to Find the Source of a Pin

- Click the image to see lots of info about the pin, including the options to pin it and send it. You'll see the boards that the image came from as well as other boards that also contain the image. You'll also find some similar pins here.
- Click the button that says **Visit site** to see where the pin came from.

How to Navigate and Search

- On the far top left side of your page, click the icon made up of three dashes in a box to see a list of categories. Click on any category to see pins on that topic.
- Next to the categories icon, you'll see a search box. After you search, click **Pins, Boards,** or **Pinners** in the upper left-hand corner of the page to narrow your results.

How to Create an Original Pin

- Find the icon that looks like a plus sign. This is located on the right side of the navigation bar. Click this to add a pin of your own. You'll see three options.
- **Upload a pin** allows you to choose an image file from your computer. This works just like attaching a file to your email.
- **Add from a website** lets you copy and paste a web address to pin an item. Just paste the URL where you found the picture and click **Find images.** Select the image and click **Pin it.**
- **Recommended Pins** shows you pins that are similar to your own.

How to View Boards and Settings

- Next to the plus-sign logo, you'll see a logo of a pin (your picture might be here if you've added one to your profile). Click this to view and edit your boards, your pins, and lots more.
- **Visit Help Center** is a great place to go if you have a question or want to learn more.
- **Settings** is the best place to go to change your password, clear your recent searches, manage the emails that Pinterest sends you, and more. Pinterest will also let you change how you sign in.
- Want to stop using Pinterest? Click **Deactivate** at the bottom of the **Settings** page.
- You should always **Log Out** in the drop-down menu under the pin.
- Finally, in the far right corner of your screen, you'll see an icon with two pins or a number. This will show you notifications. This is a great place to see new followers as well as which of your pins are the most popular.

Terms

- **Pins:** Pictures that act as visual links to websites.
- **Boards:** Collections of pins, usually organized by subject.
- **Secret Boards:** Boards that are private.
- **Pinterest Bookmarklet:** An application downloaded to your browser toolbar that allows you to easily retrieve and pin images from websites.

Resources

- **Mashable Pinterest Guide:** http://mashable.com/category/pinterest/
- **Pinterest on Pinterest:** http://about.pinterest.com/en
- **Pinterest Help Center:** http://help.pinterest.com/en

CHAPTER 5

Facebook

Facebook is a fascinating and addictive website that has literally changed the world. It's the quintessential social network—more than one billion people use the service to connect with friends, family, and things they care about. At its heart, it is simply a way to bring people all over the world together in one easy-to-use site. Facebook makes its money from ads, so the service is free for people and groups to use.

Facebook's familiarity can be a double-edged sword for teachers. It's great that everyone knows what Facebook is and what it does, but it also means that the teacher is faced with an extremely disparate skill set. Many of the people who take your class may be just as proficient on Facebook as you are. Others won't be entirely sure how to check their email. As a teacher, it's up to you to bridge the gap and offer the class at a level that can be useful for everyone. In this chapter, we'll talk about how to address privacy and safety on Facebook, as well as how it can be useful for everyone.

HOW TO PREPARE?

Facebook is simultaneously one of the most fun and most difficult social networking classes to teach. As with all the other social networking sites covered in this book, the best way to prepare is to familiarize yourself with the site by using it. Be aware that many, if not most, questions from the class will be about safety and privacy, so spend lots of time working with those settings in your own account. If you already have an account that you use fairly frequently, consider creating a second account for the purpose of teaching the class. You can then use your original account as your private account, and the new one you create as your professional one. This has lots of benefits, one of the best being that all of your students can friend you on the new account. This makes it really easy for them to send you a message asking you a question if they don't understand something.

You may want to plan a last-minute "cram session" to review Facebook right before your class. The website and app change frequently and without much warning, and this is the best way to make sure that you're prepared to address current developments. Pay special attention to the privacy and account settings, as these change often.

Many instructors teach Facebook with PowerPoint slides because it's easier to control what the patron sees that way. For example, it's difficult to ensure that none of your friends posts something objectionable that your students might see. I mitigate the possibility of this happening by using my professional account during class (former students and professional contacts only). I also take a moment during the class introduction to tell students that I cannot control the content of what they might see. I've taught thousands of students, and this has never been a problem, but the possibility is there. So, while it may be attractive to teach with PowerPoint for this reason, it really can be a disservice to your patron, because it's easy to get lost in Facebook. In Facebook, the process of how you do things is very important. There are lots of places to click, and it's easy for your patron to go astray. Doing your step-by-step instruction on a PowerPoint makes it more difficult for them to follow along. It also is harder for you in the long run, since Facebook changes so frequently that you will be constantly updating your slides.

After a number of years teaching Facebook, I finally decided in about 2010 that I would no longer do a handout. This was a big deal at my library, since we did handouts for every class at that time. The more we taught Facebook, the more we realized that it was just going to be impossible to keep up with handouts on a service that changed so frequently. Once I stopped giving out handouts, I began routinely giving out my business card and offering one-on-one sessions. Eighty percent or more of my one-on-one sessions are now for businesses or individuals that need help with Facebook. As with many of the other services we discuss in this book, I emphasize that I'd be happy to do one-on-one appointments with patrons. I often do them for account setups, privacy and security review, and page creation for community organizations and businesses.

For many people, Facebook represents social networking as a whole. As such, it can be pretty daunting—sometimes even scary. It's best to approach that issue head on. Lots of folks say that they aren't on Facebook because they're worried about their privacy and personal information. I often argue that the best way to control that information is to be active on Facebook so that you know how your information is being used. After all, you don't need to be on Facebook for a friend to upload a picture or status about you. You wouldn't even know unless someone told you or you were on Facebook yourself.

COMMON PROBLEMS IN CLASS

Probably the most frequent problem you'll run into when teaching Facebook is that Facebook is very distracting. Patrons really want to learn, and they want to follow along with you, but it's tough to focus sometimes because there's so much interesting stuff happening on their news feeds. These people often get lost and can't figure out where you are. This is no big deal! Just be prepared to frequently go back to show someone how you got to the screen you are on. You learned Facebook by playing with it, and so will they. Try to go slowly, and ask people if they're on the same page as you are as often as possible.

Many people don't think to bring their passwords with them. You can reset a password on Facebook, but that can be a bit time consuming. I've found that the best way to deal with this is to ask people to sign on to their accounts as soon as they come in. That way, you have a bit more time to work with them one on one before the class begins should that be necessary. In some cases, I have asked patrons who couldn't seem to reset passwords to just watch. I usually try to touch base with those people after the class to offer a one-on-one appointment.

POSSIBLE VARIATIONS

There are lots of different variations for types of Facebook accounts, and therefore for classes to teach. The ones you see most frequently are business accounts (which can be for professionals, for networking, or for business promotion) and accounts for groups. Both use the **Create a Page** function, which can be found on the bottom right-hand page of the main sign-in page. While it is possible to create a page without having a previous personal account, I do not suggest it. Page owners that do not have a personal account don't have the same functions available to them, which makes everything more difficult to use.

SPECIAL CONSIDERATIONS

In my years teaching many types of classes, it's been my experience that there is the widest gap of computer skills in Facebook classes. I think this is primarily because everyone has heard of Facebook, and most everyone has gotten an invite from someone they know at some time. On the flip side, the privacy settings can be daunting, so many people who are quite computer savvy come to learn about those. It can be extremely challenging to you as a teacher when you have classes with people who do not know how to check email along with those who own their own businesses, use their computers all day long, and just want to go over privacy settings. The key is to go slowly, and to offer one-on-one appointments whenever it seems that someone isn't quite keeping up with you.

One other important thing to consider is whether or not you will create accounts in the class. This is less of a problem than it used to be since so many people now have an account already, but it's important to think about. It's both time consuming and difficult to set up accounts in class, even with a volunteer to assist you. The setup forms aren't that long, but patrons must authenticate their email address before having an account that they can work with, and that can mean a significant amount of time lapses while they try to remember passwords, and so on. Instead of having students create new accounts, I recommend writing your class description to require existing accounts. If a patron seems reluctant to set up an account on their own, you can always help them do so in a one-on-one appointment.

For this reason, the handouts below omit account setup. If you really feel that you need to consider setting up accounts, you could consider splitting the intro class into two groups. The first could be for absolute beginners, the second for more advanced users. I've done this a number of times, and it does work well. Just be aware that you will probably need to recap the bulk of what you taught in the first class in the second. This doesn't necessarily need to be a deal breaker, since you should be able to do so in the first half of the class.

When you're planning for your class, you'll want to schedule about 70–80 percent of it for a Facebook tour, and the rest for privacy and account settings. These settings always take much longer to go over than you'd think, so it's good to leave some extra time for them. I ask patrons to be sure to follow along with me during this part, since we work with a number of settings that can be hard to find. I always like to emphasize that patrons should review their privacy settings every few months because Facebook frequently changes them.

INSTRUCTOR NOTES

Logistics

I generally teach Facebook in one long or two shorter sessions. Below you will find two handouts. The first is devoted to Facebook basics, while the second covers Facebook privacy. If you choose to teach the class all in one session, just hand out both guides. The Instructor Notes are not broken up into two parts, since the information that you recap in the second class will be different from group to group. If I choose to teach in one session, I plan for it to be a longer class—perhaps an hour and a half or more. I don't generally offer a break, but I do encourage people to leave early if they need to. Such a long class is unusual at my library, and I want to accommodate as many people as I can, even if it means they leave early.

The teaching script for Facebook is long and detailed. For your purposes, consider cutting out some less vital sections for your class. Of course, you may also give out the entire handout and just teach selectively from it. By providing more instead of less, you have more options with what you can teach. Feel free to edit as needed!

What Is Facebook?

- Facebook is a website and app that connects more than a billion people throughout the world. It's great for sharing pictures, life events, games, news, and lots more.
- Facebook is easy and free, and you can participate as much or as little as you'd like.

How Can Facebook Be Used?

- Facebook is a great way to keep in touch with family, colleagues, and even businesses and other organizations that interest you
- It is the perfect place for photo storage and sharing. Once upon a time, you needed to email (or mail!) pictures of the kids or grandkids to all of your relatives. With Facebook's photo capacity, you can simply upload them and choose who you'd like to be able to view them.
- In the late 1990s and early 2000s, websites like classmates.com were really hot because they helped people connect with people they hadn't known or seen in many years. Social networking sites like Facebook have largely taken the place of many of those sites. Your profile allows you to list both the schools you attended and the years you went there. It uses that information to help you find old friends and acquaintances.
- It's also a great tool for keeping up with the hottest news, trends, and the latest memes and viral videos.
- Many people use Facebook as a type of outreach. It's a fabulous forum for social causes of all kinds, as well as for businesses.
- Potential employers frequently check Facebook accounts of interviewing applicants. By having an account, you demonstrate that you're computer savvy and understand social media. Employers love this!
- Many people use Facebook as a tool for professional networking. For these individuals, Facebook is a tool for creating and maintaining business relationships.

- Facebook can also be used to set up pages for organizations. These are easily kept up to date, and can help attract new membership to a group.
- This class covers the layout of your Facebook profile, shows you how to post, respond, and share, and discusses privacy and account security concerns.

Getting Started

- To begin, go to www.facebook.com. The sign-in boxes are at the top of the page in the right-hand corner. Type your email address or username into the first box and your password into the second.
- Uncheck the box that says **Keep me logged in** if you are on a shared computer.
- Can't seem to sign in? Click the link that says **Forgot your password?** Facebook will give you several ways to reset that information.
- Once you've successfully signed in, you'll see your home page, the place where you will spend almost all of your time on Facebook.
- You should see three columns. We'll start in the upper left-hand corner and work our way down and around the page, exploring all the features of Facebook as we go.

Exploring Your Page

- Let's begin with the blue Facebook icon in the upper left-hand corner of the page. Almost every page in Facebook has this icon in the corner. It's not just for decoration or branding! If you get confused and aren't sure where you are, clicking that blue F will always take you back to your home page.

[Note to Teachers: Please note that the headings on the left side of the page can vary depending on what the student uses on Facebook.]

Your Cover Page

- Below the icon you'll see your profile picture (either a picture you uploaded or a blue outline of a person). Your name will be next to it, as well as a link to **Edit Profile**.
- Click your profile picture to see your cover page. This is the page that other people see when they search for you. As such, it's worth your attention.
- The first thing you should notice on your cover page is your profile picture and cover photo. If you don't have one, this is the place to add it. Just mouse over the profile picture until you see something that says **Update Profile Picture**. Click this link. You'll get a number

of options for using current images or uploading new ones. I usually use **Choose From Photos** or **Upload From Photos,** but any of the options will work. For this example, let's select **Choose From Photos.** A popup window will appear with your albums. The default is **Photos of You,** but you can **View Albums** on the upper right-hand corner of the popup to see the rest of your pictures. Select a photo by clicking on it. It should now appear as your profile picture.

- Does something look funny? Sometimes Facebook inadvertently cuts off important parts of your picture in an attempt to crop it to fit in such a small box. This is easy to fix! Just mouse over the image again, click **Update Profile Picture** and choose **Edit Thumbnail.** You'll be able to drag the image until it fits the given size. Click **Save** when you've finished editing.

- Now add a cover photo. Sometimes people use pictures of family or something similar, but most people use this space for a pretty picture of a sky, a skyline photo of their favorite city, or something else they find visually appealing. Most of these pictures come from Internet searches. This is okay, but please respect copyright! Creative Commons and Flickr are both great places to go to find beautiful images for your profile. Just ask the owner before using.

- Once you find your picture, save it to your computer if you haven't already. Go back to your Facebook page and mouse over the long box behind your profile picture where your cover picture will live. **Change Cover** will appear. Clicking this link will give you options to upload a picture, use a current image, or reposition. Select the appropriate action now.

- Your cover photo should now appear in the box. You might want to fix the placement. If you do, just use your mouse to click and drag where it says **Drag to Reposition Cover.** When you're done editing, just click **Save Changes** and you're done.

- The first tab of your cover page is remixed content from your profile and your news feed. Use the other tabs below your cover image to view your **Photos, Friends,** and **More.**

Photos

- In the tabs beneath your cover photo, you'll see a link for Photos. Click on this link to see photos and albums you've uploaded as well as pictures you've been tagged in.

- You'll notice right away that this page is organized into tabs on the top of the page. The page you land on will show you **Photos of You.** These are pictures that you've been tagged in. You can use the tabs to navigate to **Your Photos, Albums,** and **Not Tagged.**

- Focus on **Photos of You** first. Tagging means that you (or someone else) have indicated that you are in the picture or that it is something that is of interest to you.
- Sometimes you may find that you were incorrectly tagged in a photo, or just that you would rather not have your name on it. It's easy to untag! Just click on the picture to open it, click **Options** at the bottom of it, click **Report/Remove Tag**, and choose the box next to **I want to untag myself**. You may also click **I want this photo removed from Facebook**, although that's probably only necessary in a very small number of cases. To finish, click **Remove Tag**. The photo will still appear on Facebook, but your name will no longer be associated with it.
- Want to tag someone? That's easy, too! Just click the picture, and select **Tag Photo** at the bottom of it. Then click on the person you'd like to tag. A list of suggestions will appear, or you can just begin typing the name of the person you'd like to tag. Facebook will match what you type with the name of one of your friends. When you finish, click **Done Tagging**. Click the "X" in the corner of the picture to go back to your Photos page.
- If you'd like to add photos, there are two easy ways to do so. The first is in your status on your home page. The second is within the photos page. Click **+Create Album** to start. You'll be asked to name the album, give a location if there is one, and specify who you'd like to share it with. Once you click **Create Album**, you'll be able to upload and select the images you want to include.
- The next option, to the right of **Photos of You**, is **Your Photos**. This is a selection of images that you've uploaded to Facebook.
- There are a number of available options to work with your picture. To access those, click on the picture. The bottom will have a series of options beginning with **Tag Photo**.
- Click **Options** to see a menu that will let you change the location or date, rotate your image, set it as the profile or cover photo, move, or delete. It's especially helpful to know about this delete function, since many people often have uploader's remorse.
- **Share** will post the image on your timeline. You'll probably only want to do this if you uploaded the image via the **+Create Album** button. If the picture was uploaded because you shared it as part of your status, you obviously won't want to do so again.
- **Send** lets you type in the names of people whom you'd like to see the picture. Like the rest of Facebook, as you type, the names of your friends will appear. If you'd like to, you can add a message where it says **Write something**...
- Finally, you can **Like** your own image.

- To the right of your image, you'll see your profile picture indicating that you uploaded it. You'll also see anything that you wrote, as well as any comments or likes that the picture has.
- To leave the screen with your enlarged photo, just click the **X** in the upper right-hand corner.
- Back on your main photos page, the next option to the right of **Your Photos** is **Albums**. Here you'll see all the albums you created, or that were created for you by Facebook. You can create a new one here, as well as edit an entire album at one time. To do this, click the name of the album. In the right-hand corner, you'll see an option that says **Edit**. Click this and you'll be able to tag people, edit descriptions, delete photos, move to a different album, or make the image your album cover.
- Finally, you'll see something that says **Not Tagged**. This is located to the right of **Albums**. Here you can add tags to anything that might be missing one.

Friends

- The tab next to **Photos** under your cover photo is for **Friends**. This page is a helpful list of your friends.
- Mouse over **Friends** after each name to add friends to groups.
- If you'd no longer like to be friends with someone, click **Unfriend** from the drop-down menu. You will no longer see notifications from this person, and they will not see your updates. When you unfriend someone, they are not notified.
- Use the search box on the right-hand side of the page to find more friends.
- **Friend Requests** are also located on the right side of this page.

More

- The **More** tab is useful for finding and managing your interests on Facebook. To use this tab, select a category from the drop-down menu.

Editing Your Profile

- Click on the blue **F** in the upper left-hand corner to return to your main page.
- Now take a moment to find and update your profile information.
- A few moments ago, you saw **Edit Profile** located next to the profile picture on your main page. Click that link now.

- The page you'll see is similar to the cover page, but if you scroll down, you'll see lots of ways to input and update your information. You'll see lots of blanks for education, relationships, basic information, and much more. This information will be public to one degree or another, so put in only the information you are comfortable sharing with your friends and the world!
- To edit or update your information, find the section you'd like to work with and click the **Edit** button next to it. You'll see a drop-down menu where you can select your updated information easily. When you're done, just click **Save**.
- Click on the blue F in the upper left-hand corner to go back to your main page.

Your News Feed

- Now go back to the left side of the main page again. Underneath the profile picture, you should see something that says **News Feed**. It will be highlighted in blue. Your news feed is the posts and pictures from your friends on Facebook that are located in the center of the page, as well as content that you submit. This will be a combination of pictures, links, and plain-text posts.
- At the top of your news feed, you'll see a long skinny box with **What's on your mind?** in it. This is where you type your status updates. Just type in your update and click **Post**, and your message will appear in the news feeds of your friends.
- Want to add pictures or video instead? Just click the **Add Photos/ Video** link. You'll be prompted to select the file you'd like to share from your computer.
- As you look through the status updates from your friends, you will be able to comment, like, or share them. Just look for the blue links under each post, picture, or video.
- To write a message, click the **Comment** button or simply type in the box that says **Write a comment** ... Hit enter to send. Remember that when you comment on something, your friends will see that message as well as the friends of the person that you are writing to.
- If you'd like to add a picture to your comment, just click the camera icon inside the comment box.
- Click **Like** if you think something is great but don't necessarily want to comment on it. Many people both like and comment on a status, and that's totally okay, too.
- **Share** will copy the post from the news feed of the friend and add it to your own. Once you share a post, all of your friends will see it too.

- As you scroll through your news feed, you'll see a number of **Promoted Posts**. These are essentially ads and you do not need to click on them if you aren't interested. You can't get rid of these, but you can control to some degree what will appear in them. More on this in a bit.
- You may also see something called a **Suggested Post**. This isn't necessarily an ad; sometimes Facebook suggests pages you might like in this way. Feel free to ignore these, too. If you want to see more content from the promoted page, just click **Like Page** above it.

Messages

- Back on the left side of the page, look for **Messages** under News Feed. Click the word, and it will take you to a page where you can send and receive what is essentially Facebook email.
- Please note that aside from chat, this is the only private message on Facebook.
- To send a private message, click +**New Message**, located in the upper right-hand corner of the middle pane. A new page will appear, with your cursor already in the **To** box. As you start to type the name, a drop-down will appear with the matching name of your friend. Just click the name to select the person. Once you've selected your friend or friends, click inside the box below that says **Write a message**... Type your message here and click **Send**. When your friend replies, you'll receive a notification and you can reply in the same place.
- If you want to see any older messages from any of your friends, those will appear on the left side of the page. Like your regular email, you can click on any of these to read and respond to them.
- When you're done reading and responding to your messages, click the blue F in the upper left-hand corner to return to your home page.

Events

- Back on the left side of your home page, you should see **Events** listed underneath messages.
- Events are great for inviting people to a party or event, to like a cause, and lots more. A number next to the word **Events** on the left side of the page indicates you've been invited to something.
- If you've been invited to something, the invitation will appear at the top of the page. Click on the title in blue to see more information about the event. You can click **Join, Maybe,** or **Hide** to reply. When you join, or indicate you'll be attending, the person who set up the event will be notified. There will also be a wall, or a place you can

comment, on the event page. Other attendees and people who have been invited are generally listed in that area as well.

- The Events section is also a terrific place to find a listing of upcoming birthdays.
- Want to host your own event? Just click +**Create Event** in the upper right-hand corner of the page. You'll be prompted to select the friends you'd like to invite and write the event information. After you've created it, the friends you've invited will receive a notification so that they may respond.
- When you're finished with **Events**, click the blue F in the upper left-hand corner to return to your home page.

Find Friends

- **Find Friends** shows you new friend requests. It also has a handy feature called **People You May Know**. This is a list of people who are friends with your friends, went to school with you, or are otherwise connected with you in some way. The more information Facebook has about you, the better these recommendations get. Browse through them now. If you see someone you'd like to connect with, click the **Add Friend** button next to their name. If you'd like to see more about them before doing this, just click their name.
- On the right side of the page, you'll see a box that says **Add Personal Contacts**. This feature pulls contacts from your personal email and sends them friend requests on Facebook. It's up to you if you'd like to do this. Many people do find it a bit invasive.
- Click the blue F icon to get back to your home page.

Apps

- You have several options in the **Apps** section of Facebook.
- **Games** is where you can find any invites from friends for games. You'll also see a selection of the most popular games sorted by popularity and type.
- **Pokes** are a way of saying "hi" to a friend. You aren't necessarily saying anything in particular; it's just a way to tell someone you're thinking of them. Clicking on this option lets you see who has poked you, and allows you to poke others.
- **Games Feed** shows you what your friends are playing right now.

Groups

- This category has different options for everyone. If you've joined a group, it'll be listed here. At the bottom of the list, everyone should have an option that says **Create Group**. This does exactly what you'd think! It's good for sharing similar interests and causes.

Pages

- Pages are generally put up by a group, business, or organization to represent themselves and share important information. Liking a page is a great way to keep up to date with the group.
- If you are an admin on a page, the name of the page will be listed here. Clicking on it will take you to the page.
- **Like Pages** shows you a suggested list of pages to follow. It also shows you invites from your friends. You can review these as suggestions. For example, if you and I are friends and we both like to camp, I might suggest that you'd like to follow the National Park Service pages.
- **Create a Page** ... helps you to set up a page for your group or organization. It's easy, and you can designate other people (called admins) to post content and manage the page.

Friends

- Under **Friends**, there are listings of groups. These are different for everyone, but will usually be under the names of your town and the schools you've attended. Each name has a number after it. Clicking each of these takes you to the friends who are part of that network.

Navigation Bar

- The dark blue bar running across the top of the page is referred to as your navigation bar. Here you can search, see your notifications, and access your profile and privacy settings.

[Note: Teachers, when you demonstrate the Navigation Bar, consider having your students search for your library and Like the page. It's even better if you can have them search for you, too. That way they have experience searching for places and people. You may even want them to add you as a friend. This has several advantages. Once they add you, you'll be connected on Facebook and they can easily ask you questions. Also, your students will see what a friend request looks like as you receive theirs. If they have trouble finding you by name (sometimes this happens), suggest that they find you by your email address.]

Search

- The search box can be found directly to the right of the blue "F" Facebook icon that you've been using to return to your home page.

Click inside this box to search for people, places, things, groups, and lots more.

- Click on the box now and start typing in a search. For now, let's search for the library.
- As you type, you'll notice that Facebook tries to match what you're typing with a place or account. When your desired search term appears, just click on it to see the page.
- Once you've found the account, you can easily send a friend request or like a page by clicking on the appropriate button on the profile.

Notifications

- To the right of your search box, you'll notice a series of three icons. If there is a red number over any of these icons, it means that you have a notification, or something that you might like to know about. Click on the icon to see the notifications in a list. Each item can be clicked on to see more.
- The first icon that you'll see is that of two people side by side. This is your notification for friend requests. When someone searches for you and sends you a request on Facebook, the notification appears here. Just click on this icon to confirm or ignore the request.
- The second icon is two thought bubbles. This is a second place to receive messages on Facebook. When you click the icon, it takes you to the same page as the **Messages** option on the left side of the screen does. Here you can send and receive messages from any of your friends.
- The final icon is a globe. It is for general notifications. You'll see a number here when someone likes your status, comments on a picture, or does just about anything else on your page.

Shortcuts

- To the right of the icons, you'll find a few handy shortcuts.
- **Your name** will be the first shortcut. That will take you to your cover page.
- **Home** does the same thing as the blue Facebook icon. It takes you to your home page.
- **Find Friends** is a shortcut that takes you to the same page as the **Find Friends** on the left side of the screen.
- The combination lock is a shortcut to some of your privacy pages. We'll explore those in a moment.

Account Security and Privacy Settings

- The final icon on the blue bar is a down arrow. This takes you to your account and privacy settings. Click the icon to see a drop-down menu of options.
- First, click **Settings**. This brings you to your **General Account Settings**. This page works much the same way as your regular page does—each item on the left side shows different content in the middle.

General Account Settings

- Start now with **General Account Settings**. Click **Edit** next to each item you'd like to change. We won't cover all of these, but there are a few that are great to know about.
- Clicking **Edit** next to **Name** takes you to a page where you can change your name and choose an alternate name. This is great for women who would like to change their names after marriage, or would like to include their maiden names in their account information. To save the settings, you will need to enter a password. Be aware that you may only change your name a few times during the life of your account. Be sure it's correct the first time!
- You may also like to choose a new **Username**. Clicking into this section will let you change how you sign into Facebook, and will replace the generic URL of your home page with a URL including your name. The username can only be changed once, and should include your name. When you're done, click **Save Changes**.
- **Email** will let you change your email for notifications.
- Need to change your password? Just click on **Password** and follow the prompts.

Security

- Clicking **Security** takes you to **Security Settings**, a list of options that you can use to more closely safeguard your account.
- **Login Notifications** sends you a message any time your account is accessed on a device or computer that you've never used before. This can help you to determine earlier if your account has been hacked. If you'd like to enable this feature, just choose the checkbox next to the method of notification method of choice. When you're done, click **Save Changes**.
- **Login Approvals** sends a security code to your phone each time your account is logged into from a different browser.

- **Code Generator** works with login approvals to provide you access to your account faster.
- **App Passwords** lets you bypass login approvals for apps like Skype or Spotify.
- **Trusted Contacts** are sent a code that can help you log in to your account if you ever forget the password or are locked out.
- **Trusted Browsers** is another layer of security for your login. It lists both devices and browsers that have been used to access your account.
- **Active Sessions** lists the locations from where you've logged in.
- If you ever decide you'd no longer like to be on Facebook, you can find the link for this at the bottom of this page. Just click on **Deactivate your account** and follow the prompts.

Privacy

- Now let's discuss the settings within the privacy tab on the left side of the page. The options on this page are fairly self-explanatory. You'll see three categories, each with a series of questions. To change each option, just click it. In most cases you'll be able to use a drop-down menu to change your preference.
- Under **Who can see my stuff?** you'll see three questions. Your choices for each will be up to you and your comfort level with Facebook.
  - The first question, **Who can see your future posts?** determines who can view each item that you post. Keep in mind that you can also change this manually when you post.
  - **Review all your posts and things you're tagged in** shows you items that your friends posted your name in connection with.
  - The final option, **Limit the audience for posts you've shared with friends of friends or Public,** will restrict older postings so that they're viewable by friends only.
- The next category is **Who can contact me?**
  - Under the first question, **Who can send you friend requests?** it will be up to you to determine how visible you wish to be on Facebook. You'll be able to choose **Everyone** or **Friends of Friends** here.
  - The next option, **Whose messages do I want filtered into my Inbox?** might be helpful for you to know about if you find yourself getting spam on a regular basis. Spam is pretty unusual on Facebook, but it does happen. This option will filter based on people you might know versus messages from friends. To choose one, just click the circle in front of it.

- **Who can look me up?** is an option because sometimes it can be tough to find someone by their name. With over a billion people, there are likely to be a number with any given name. Instead of using your name, the person trying to find you may use your email address instead. This setting determines who can do that.
  - **Who can look you up using the phone number you provided?** is similar. There probably isn't much need to have your phone number on Facebook in the first place.
- The final question, **Do you want other search engines to link to your timeline?** allows search engines to find your profile and display it to people who may search for you. This won't supersede the privacy controls you have set up. If you choose to set your privacy so that only your friends can see much of your information, someone searching for you who isn't your friend should not see that information.

Timeline and Tagging

- This section helps you control the content that appears in your timeline, and it allows you to determine how friends may indicate that particular content is about you.
- **Timeline and Tagging** is set up in much the same way as **Privacy**. Just answer a series of questions to set your controls.
- The first category is **Who can add things to my timeline?**
  - Under **Who can post to your timeline?** you can choose **Friends** or **Only Me** from the drop-down menu.
  - Under this, you'll see **Review posts friends tag you in before they appear on your timeline?** This is an option that can be turned off and on. If you're concerned about what other people might say or post about you, this is a great setting to know about. If you turn this on, you'll be notified anytime this happens and will need to approve the content before it becomes live on your own profile.
- The next section lets you determine **Who can see things on your timeline?** Click **Review what other people see on your timeline.** This gives you a preview of how you've done with your privacy controls. The page you'll see is how your timeline looks, either to the public or to a specific person. The next option, **Who can see posts you've been tagged in on your timeline?** does just what it sounds like. You have a wide range of groups to choose from in this setting. Just choose the one that is comfortable for you in the drop down menu. Finally, **Who can see what others post on your timeline?** gives you that same wide range of options.

- The final section, **How can I manage tags people add and tagging suggestions?** gives you the opportunity to review how tags are used on your profile.
  - The first question, **Review tags people add to your own posts before the tags appear on Facebook?** will let you review when a friend has tagged you in your own content.
  - When you're tagged in a post, who do you want to add to the audience if they aren't already in it? will allow you to choose **Friends, Only Me,** or **Custom.** Custom is a great option, because it can let you add particular people or groups, or exclude them as well.
  - Finally, **Who sees tag suggestions when photos that look like you are uploaded?** gives you the option of choosing **Friends** or **No One.** Facebook has advanced facial recognition software and can often place a name with a picture. In this setting, you'll be able to control whether you'll allow them to do so.

Blocking

- **Blocking** is one of the most helpful tools in your privacy settings. You can block people, apps, events, and more.
- **Restricted List** designates particular friends that can see only information that is available to the public on your page. This is helpful if you aren't ready to unfriend someone but would still like to limit that person's access to your information.
- **Block Users** is ideal for people who may harass you or bother you on Facebook. To block someone, just type their name in the box provided. Choose the name from the drop-down menu and click **Block.** This action severs the relationship between the two of you. The person will no longer be able to see your activity or interact with you in any way. They will not get a notification that they've been blocked. After you've added someone to your blocked list, you can remove them by clicking **Unblock** next to their name.
- **Block app invites** is fantastic for blocking app invites from those users that constantly send you gaming and other invites that don't interest you. You'll see their other content; you just won't see any of the requests. Again, the person won't know you've done this.
- **Block event invites** does the same thing. This will limit all of the invites you see from a particular person. Just type in the name of the person to block.
- **Block apps** is a fabulous setting to know about. If you're sick of Candy Crush Saga or Mafia Wars, just type in the name and the app will no longer be able to use your information.

Notification Settings

- **Notifications** are great to review if you'd like to specify what Facebook may or may not contact you about. This includes notifications by email. To review each setting, click the line it's located on. You'll be able to turn the notification on and off. If you're the most interested in managing your email notifications, that's under **Email**, under **How You Get Notifications**.
- **What You Get Notified About** allows you to determine which actions are important enough for you to get contacted about. All of these settings can be adjusted or turned off completely.

Mobile

- If you don't have a smartphone with the Facebook app, you can use the **Mobile** tab to add a phone number. You'll get notifications from Facebook when there is activity on your account. Facebook does not charge for this service, but your cell service provider will charge for the messages you receive, so use this feature with caution.

Followers

- **Followers** is a newer option on Facebook. Enabling this setting allows people to follow your public profile without actually becoming your friend. Check the box if you'd like to enable this option. This might be a useful way to keep up with colleagues or professional contacts.

Apps

- This page lists apps that have permission to access any of your content. Some of your profile elements will always be available to the public, as well as the list of your current Facebook friends.
- To remove any of your apps, just click the **X** at the end of the line they're listed on. When you delete the app, you'll have the option to delete all of your Facebook activity related to it. Just check the box provided.
- If you'd like to learn more about how the app uses your information, click **Edit**. You'll see who sees your activity, permissions that you've given the app, when you last used it, and legal information. You can also change how and when the app sends you notifications here.

- Below the listing of your apps, you'll see a few more settings.
  - ○ **Apps others use** determines the amount and type of your information that other people can take with you into apps they use. It's nice to provide a bit of information because sometimes mutual friends are able to contact you this way; but it's good to keep this minimal. In my personal account, I include my name, my birthplace, and my current city. Everyone is different, though, so do what works for you. Just check the boxes next to the information that you are okay with providing.
  - ○ If you'd like to, you can restrict all of the content that your friends take with you into other apps. Be aware that if you do this, you will not be able to use any apps yourself.
  - ○ **Instant personalization** sends your information forward to particular partner websites so that you may interact with your friends on them. Many people like to turn this feature off since it can feel invasive. To do so, just click **Instant personalization**, then uncheck the box that says **Enable instant personalization on partner websites.**
  - ○ Finally, you'll see something that says **Old versions of Facebook for mobile.** This can be helpful to you if you're using an old mobile app that doesn't let you restrict audience post by post. Just use the dropdown menu to choose the default of who you would like to share with.

Ads

- Facebook is supported by ads, so you'll always see them. The settings on this page let you determine how your information is used for ads, as well as the type of ads you see (to some extent).
- **Third Party Sites** is where you can turn off the ability for Facebook to provide your information to third-party vendors so that they can use it for ads. This is not something that Facebook currently does, but according to its terms and conditions, it could do so at any time. To decline permission for Facebook to do this, click **Edit.** Look for **If we allow this in the future, show my information to.** In the dropdown box, choose **No one,** then click **Save Changes.**
- **Ads and Friends** deals with what your friends see in their ads based on your personal information. If I had this setting turned on, I could reasonably expect that my liking a store that sells cat products might lead to ads for kitty litter or collars on the pages of my friends. This happens because Facebook figures that you share interests with your friends, so it advertises according to your interests. To turn this

setting off, click **Edit**. Look for **Pair my social actions with ads for**. Use the drop-down menu to choose **No one**. When you're done, click **Save Changes**.

- **Website and Mobile App Custom Audiences** controls cookies (or packets of information that a website stores about you to customize your experience on their page). These can be sent to Facebook from partnering sites for advertising purposes. To turn these off, look for **Opt out** in blue. It's a tiny link located under **Learn more**. The next page has lots of information on this. To turn it off, look for the **Opt out button** located in the middle of the page. Know that if you use multiple browsers (Firefox, Internet Explorer, etc.) and different computers to access Facebook, you'll need to repeat this on each, since the setting only works within the browser you are currently using. A popup box will appear asking you if you'd like to opt out. Click **Submit** to save the setting. If you clear your cookies on a particular browser, you will need to opt out again.
- To return to your privacy settings, click the arrow in the far right-hand corner. Select **Settings**.

Payments

- **Payments** lets you determine how you'd like to pay for in-app purchases, gift cards, and more if you choose to do so.

Support Dashboard

- If you're having technical problems with Facebook, check out **Support Dashboard** to see the status of any problems you've reported.

Additional Settings

- Now return to the arrow at the upper right-hand corner of the page. We'll take a brief moment here to run over the other options located here.
- Under **Settings**, you'll see the link to **Log Out**. If you share a computer, you always log out when you're finished with your Facebook session.
- Next you'll see the option for **Help**. Clicking this takes you to a support page with searchable questions and answers. If this doesn't solve your problem, use the final link under the arrow, **Report a Problem**.

Chat

- Finally, look to the bottom right-hand corner of your screen. You'll see a box with the names of a few of your friends. This feature shows you who is online at any given moment. By clicking on any of these names, you'll start a real-time conversation with that friend.
- Sometimes you'd like to browse Facebook without having the chat feature on. Just click the gear at the bottom of the box and select **Turn Off Chat**. Now your friends will not see when you are online.

Closing

That's it! You now know how to use Facebook like a pro. Please feel free to contact us with any questions.

FACEBOOK ESSENTIALS

What Is Facebook?

- Facebook is a website and app that connects more than a billion people throughout the world. It's great for sharing pictures, life events, games, news, and lots more.

How Can Facebook Be Used?

- Facebook is a great way to keep in touch with family, colleagues, and even businesses and other organizations that interest you. It's also terrific for keeping up with the hottest news, trends, and the latest memes and viral videos. It's perfect for social causes and outreach, too.
- This class covers the layout of your Facebook profile, shows you how to post, respond, and share, and discusses privacy and account security concerns.

How to Get Started

- To begin, go to www.facebook.com. The sign-in boxes are at the top of the page in the right-hand corner. Type your email address or username into the first box and your password into the second. Uncheck the box that says **Keep me logged in** if you are on a shared computer.
- If you need it, the **Forgot your password?** link is located below the sign-in boxes.

How to Access and Edit Your Profile

- Below the icon, you'll see your profile picture (either a picture you uploaded or a blue outline of a person). Your name will be next to it, as well as a link to **Edit Profile**.
- Click your profile picture to see your cover page. If you don't have a profile or cover picture, this is the place to add them. Mouse over the empty box and follow the prompts to upload and edit your image, or use one you've already added.
- To update your information, click on the F in the upper left-hand corner. Click **Edit Profile** located next to the profile picture on your main page.
- To edit or update your information, find the section you'd like to work with and click the **Edit** button next to it. You'll see a drop-down menu where you can select your updated information easily. When you're done, just click **Save**. Remember to add only information that you are comfortable sharing.

Posting to Your News Feed

- Your news feed is the stream of picture, link, and text posts located in the center of your main page. At the top of your news feed you'll see a long skinny box with the text **What's on your mind?** This is where you type your status updates. Just type in your message and click **Post**, and your message will appear in the news feeds of your friends.

(continued)

From *Teaching Social Media: The Can-Do Guide* by Liz Kirchhoff.
Santa Barbara, CA: Libraries Unlimited. Copyright © 2014.

- **Add Photos/Video** will prompt you to select the file you'd like to share from your computer.

Interacting with Friends

- As you look through the status updates from your friends, you will be able to comment, like, or share them. Just look for the blue links under each post, picture, or video.
- To write a message, click the **Comment** button or simply type in the box that says **Write a comment** ... Hit enter to send. Remember that when you comment on something, your friends will see that message as well as the friends of the person that you are writing to. Add a picture by clicking the camera icon.
- Click **Like** if you think something is great but don't necessarily want to comment on it.
- **Share** will copy the post from the news feed of the friend and add it to your own. Once you share a post, all of your friends will see it, too.
- As you scroll through your news feed, you'll see a number of **Promoted Posts** and **Suggested Posts**. These are ads and suggestions from Facebook.

Send a Private Message

- Back on the left side of the main page, click **Messages** to go to Facebook email.
- To send a private message, click **+New Message**, located in the upper right-hand corner of the middle pane. Add the name of the recipient and the message in the appropriate boxes and click **Send**. When your friend replies, you'll receive a notification, and you can reply in the same place.

View and Respond to Events

- Back on the left side of your home page, click **Events** listed underneath **Messages**.
- If you see a number next to the word **Events** on the left side of the page that means you've been invited to a party or event, or someone has suggested that you support a cause.
- Click on the title in blue to see more and respond to the invitation.
- The Events section is also a terrific place to find a listing of upcoming birthdays.
- Click **+Create Event** in the upper right-hand corner of the page to make your own invite. You'll be prompted to select the friends you'd like to invite and write the event information. The invitation will be sent, and will show up as a notification for those included.

Work with Photos

- On your cover page, you'll see a link for **Photos**. Click on this link to see photos and albums you've uploaded as well as pictures you've been tagged in.

- You'll notice right away that this page is organized into tabs on the top of the page. The page you land on will show you**Photos of You**. These are pictures that you've been tagged in. You can use the tabs to navigate to **Your Photos, Albums,** and **Not Tagged**.
- Tagging means that you have (or someone else has) indicated that you are in the picture or that it is something of interest to you. To untag, just click on the picture to open it, click **Options** at the bottom of it, click **Report/ Remove Tag**, and choose the box next to **I want to untag myself**. You may also click **I want this photo removed from Facebook**. To finish, click **Remove Tag**.
- To tag someone, click the picture, and select **Tag Photo**. Then click on the person you'd like to tag. Facebook will match what you begin to type here with the name of one of your friends. When you finish, click **Done Tagging**.
- Click **+Create Album** to add new photos. You'll be asked to name the album, give a location if there is one, and specify who you'd like to share it with. Click **Create Album** to upload and select the images to include.
- There are a number of available options to work with your picture. To access those, click on the picture. The bottom will have a series of options beginning with **Tag Photo**.
- Click **Options** to see a menu that will let you change the location or date, rotate your image, set it as the profile or cover photo, or move or delete it.
- **Share** will post the image on your timeline, while **Send** lets you type in the names of people whom you'd like to see the picture.
- Finally, you can **Like** your own image.
- Back on your main photos page, the next option to the right of **Your Photos** is **Albums**. You can create or edit an entire album at one time. To do this, click the name of the album. Click **Edit** and you'll be able to tag people, edit descriptions, delete photos, move to a different album, or make the image your album cover.
- Finally, click **Not Tagged** to add tags to images that have none.

Find Friends

- **Find Friends** shows you new friend requests and helps you to send new ones. **People You May Know** is a list of people who are friends with your friends, went to school with you, or are otherwise connected with you in some way. If you see someone you'd like to connect with, click **Add Friend**.
- **Add Personal Contacts** pulls contacts from your personal mail and sends them friend requests on Facebook.

Find Your Groups

- This category has different options for everyone. If you've joined a group, it'll be listed here. At the bottom of the list, everyone should have an option that says **Create Group**. This does exactly what you'd think! It's good for sharing similar interests and causes.

(continued)

See Your Friends

- Under **Friends**, there are listings of groups. These are different for everyone, but will usually be under the names of your town and the schools you've attended. Each name has a number after it. Clicking each of these takes you to the friends who are part of that network.

Search

- To search, look for the long skinny box at the top of the page. Click here to search for people, places, things, groups, and lots more.
- Click on the box now and start typing in a search. For now, let's search for the library.
- As you type, you'll notice that Facebook tries to match what you're typing with a place or account. When your desired search term appears, just click on it to see the page.
- Once you've found the account, you can easily send a friend request or like a page by clicking on the appropriate button on the profile.

Viewing Notifications

- To the right of your search box, you'll notice a series of three icons. If there is a red number over any of these icons, it means that you have a notification. Click on the icon to see the notifications in a list. Each item can be clicked on for details.
- The first icon that you'll see is that of two people side by side. This is your notification for friend requests. Just click on this icon to confirm or ignore the request.
- The second icon is two thought bubbles. When you click the icon, it takes you to your **Messages** page.
- The final icon is a globe. It is for general notifications. You'll see a number here when someone likes your status, comments on a picture, or does just about anything else on your page.

Accessing Account Security and Privacy Settings

- Start by clicking the arrow icon within the blue bar. This takes you to your account and privacy settings.
- **Account Settings** brings you to your **General Account Settings**. Use the menu on the left side of the page to review your privacy and account settings in the middle of the page.

Chat with Friends

- **Chat** shows you who is online at any given moment. Click on any of these names located in the bottom right-hand corner of your main page to start a real-time conversation with a friend.
- To appear offline, just click the gear in the bottom of the box, and select **Turn Off Chat**.

From *Teaching Social Media: The Can-Do Guide* by Liz Kirchhoff.
Santa Barbara, CA: Libraries Unlimited. Copyright © 2014.

How to Log Out

- Click the arrow icon in the upper right-hand corner of the page.
- Under **Settings**, you'll see the link to **Log Out**. If you share a computer, you should always log out when you're finished with your Facebook session.

Terms

- **News feed:** The stream of posts, comments, images, and other media in the middle of your home page. This includes your posts as well as those from your friends.
- **Friend:** A person you have chosen to connect with on Facebook. This is a reciprocal relationship.
- **Follow:** Allows you to see updates about someone without actually becoming friends with them.
- **Block:** Severs a relationship with a person. Also can block invites, app requests, and other unwanted content.
- **Like:** A thumbs-up, or positive feedback about something.
- **Notifications:** Updates about activity on your content and activities.
- **Poke:** A quick way to say "hi" to a friend.
- **Timeline:** This is a list of your posts, events, milestones, and more.
- **Wall:** The area of your timeline where your friends can post content.

Resources

- **Mashable Facebook Guide:** http://mashable.com/category/facebook/
- **Facebook Help Center:** https://www.facebook.com/help/

FACEBOOK PRIVACY ESSENTIALS

Sharing Appropriately

- The first step in controlling your privacy is evaluating what you share in the first place. Might what you are about to post be eventually embarrassing? Could it possibly make someone feel bad? Does it share more than you would like the world to know? When you answer these questions, remember that most of what you post online never really goes away. It's possible (perhaps even likely) that future employers will see what you are about to say.

Account Security and Privacy Settings

- To access your privacy and account, click **Settings**. You can find these by clicking on the arrow located in the blue bar on the top of the page. This brings you to your **General Account Settings**. This page works much the same way as your regular page does—each item on the left side shows different content in the middle.

General Account Settings

- Start now with **General Account Settings**. Click **Edit** next to each item you'd like to change. You can edit your name, your username, your email, and lots more here. Be sure to save your changes.
- Need to change your password? Just click on **Password** and follow the prompts.

Security

- Clicking **Security** takes you to **Security Settings**, a list of options that you can use to more closely safeguard your account.
- **Login Notifications** sends you a message anytime your account is accessed on a device or computer that you've never used before. This can help you to determine earlier if your account has been hacked. If you'd like to enable this feature, just choose the checkbox next to the notification method of choice. When you're done, click **Save Changes**.
- **Login Approvals** sends a security code to your phone each time your account is logged into from a different browser.
- **Code Generator** works with login approvals to provide you access to your account faster.
- **App Passwords** lets you bypass login approvals for apps like Skype or Spotify.
- **Trusted Contacts** are sent a code that can help you log in to your account if you ever forget the password or are locked out.
- **Trusted Browsers** is another layer of security for your login. It includes a list of devices that have accessed your account.
- **Where You're Logged In** lists the locations where you've logged in from.
- If you ever decide you'd no longer like to be on Facebook, you can find the link for this at the bottom of this page. Just click on **Deactivate your account** and follow the prompts. Deactivating your account means that it will disappear from Facebook. Because the information is still saved with Facebook,

From *Teaching Social Media: The Can-Do Guide* by Liz Kirchhoff.
Santa Barbara, CA: Libraries Unlimited. Copyright © 2014.

you can log back in anytime to reactivate your account. If you'd like to delete your account forever, you must email Facebook to do so.

Privacy

- Now let's discuss the settings within the privacy tab on the left side of the page. You'll see three categories, each with a series of questions. To change each option, just click it and use the drop-down menu to change your preferences.
- Under **Who can see my stuff?** you'll see three questions. Your choices for each will be up to you and your comfort level with Facebook.
  - ○ The first question, **Who can see your future posts?** determines who can view each item that you post. This can also be changed manually when you post.
  - ○ **Review all your posts and things you're tagged in** shows you items that your friends posted your name in connection with.
  - ○ **Limit the audience for posts you've shared with friends of friends or Public** will restrict older postings so that they're viewable by friends only.
- The next category is **Who can contact me?**
  - ○ Under the first question, **Who can send you friend requests?** it will be up to you to determine how visible you wish to be on Facebook. Choose **Everyone** or **Friends of Friends** here.
  - ○ The next option, **Whose messages do I want filtered into my Inbox?** might be helpful for you to know about if you find yourself getting spam on a regular basis. This option will filter based on people you might know versus messages from friends. To choose one, just click the circle in front of it.
- **Who can look me up?** lets you determine who may search for you by email address.
  - ○ **Who can look you up using the phone number you provided?** is similar. There probably isn't much need to have your phone number on Facebook in the first place.
  - ○ The final question—**Do you want other search engines to link to your timeline?**—allows search engines to find your profile and display it to people who may search for you. This won't supersede the privacy controls you have already set up.

Timeline and Tagging

- **Timeline and Tagging** is set up in much the same way as **Privacy** is. Just answer a series of questions to set your preferences.
- The first category is **Who can add things to my timeline?**
  - ○ Under **Who can post to your timeline?** you can choose **Friends** or **Only Me** from the drop-down menu.
  - ○ **Review posts friends tag you in before they appear on your timeline?** gives you the option to approve posts that mention you before they go live on your timeline.

(continued)

From *Teaching Social Media: The Can-Do Guide* by Liz Kirchhoff.
Santa Barbara, CA: Libraries Unlimited. Copyright © 2014.

- The next section lets you determine **Who can see things on your timeline?** Click **Review what other people see on your timeline.** The page you'll see is how your timeline looks to either the public or to a specific person. The next option is **Who can see posts you've been tagged in on your timeline?** You have a wide range of groups available to choose from in this setting. Just choose the one that is comfortable for you in the drop-down menu. Finally, **Who can see what others post on your timeline?** gives you that same wide range of options.
- The final section—**How can I manage tags people add and tagging suggestions?**—gives you the opportunity to review how tags are used on your profile.
  - The first question, **Review tags people add to your own posts before the tags appear on Facebook?** will let you review when a friend has tagged you in your own content.
  - **When you're tagged in a post, who do you want to add to the audience if they aren't already in it?** will allow you to choose **Friends, Only Me,** or **Custom.** Custom is a great option, because it can let you add particular people or groups, or exclude them as well.
  - Finally, **Who sees tag suggestions when photos that look like you are uploaded?** gives you the option of choosing **Friends** or **No One.** Facebook has advanced facial recognition software and can often place a name with a picture. In this setting, you'll be able to control whether you'll allow them to do so.

Blocking

- Blocking is one of the most helpful tools in your privacy settings. You can block people, apps, events, and more.
- **Restricted List** designates particular friends that can only see information that is available to the public on your page.
- **Block Users** is ideal for people who may harass you or bother you on Facebook. To block someone, just type their name in the box provided. Choose the name from the drop-down menu and click **Block.** This action severs the relationship between the two of you. The person will no longer be able to see your activity or interact with you in any way. They will not get a notification that they've been blocked. After you've added someone to your blocked list, you can remove them by clicking **Unblock** next to their name.
- **Block app invites** is fantastic for blocking app invites from those users that constantly send you gaming and other invites that you aren't interested in. You'll still see their other content; you just won't see any of the requests. Again, the person won't know you've done this.
- **Block event invites** does the same thing. This will limit all of the invites you see from a particular person. Just type in the name of the person to block.
- **Block apps** is a fabulous setting to know about. If you're sick of Candy Crush Saga or Mafia Wars, just type in the name and the app will no longer be able to use your information.

Notification Settings

- **Notifications** help you to set what Facebook can notify you about. To review each setting, click the line it's located on. You'll be able to turn the notification on and off. If you're more interested in managing your email notifications, go to **Email** under **How You Get Notifications**.
- **What You Get Notified About** allows you to determine which actions are important enough for you to get contacted about. All of these settings can be adjusted or turned off completely.

Mobile

- If you don't have a smartphone with the Facebook app, you can use the **Mobile** tab to add a phone number. You'll get notifications from Facebook when there is activity on your account. Facebook does not charge for this service, but your cell service provider will charge for the messages you receive, so use this feature with caution.

Followers

- **Followers** is a newer option on Facebook. It allows people to follow your public profile without actually becoming your friend. Check the box if you'd like to enable this.

Manage Your Apps

- This page lists apps that have permission to access any of your content. To remove any of your apps, just click the **X** at the end of the line they're listed on. When you delete the app, you may also delete all your activity. Just check the box provided.
- If you'd like to learn more about how the app uses your information, click **Edit**. You'll see who sees your activity, permissions that you've given the app, when you last used it, and legal information. You can also change how and when the app sends you notifications here.
- Below the listing of your apps, you'll see a few more settings.
- **Apps others use** determines the amount and type of your information that other people can take with you into apps they use. Just check the boxes next to the information that you are okay with providing. If you'd like to, you can restrict all of the content that your friends take with you into other apps. Be aware that if you do this, you will not be able to use any apps yourself.
- **Instant personalization** sends your information forward to particular partner websites so that you may interact with your friends on them. Many people like to turn this feature off. To do so, just click **Instant personalization**, then uncheck the box that says **Enable instant personalization on partner websites**.
- Finally, you'll see something that says **Old versions of Facebook for mobile**. This can be helpful if you're using an old mobile app that doesn't let you restrict audience post by post. Just use the drop-down menu to choose the default of who you would like to share with.

(continued)

From *Teaching Social Media: The Can-Do Guide* by Liz Kirchhoff.
Santa Barbara, CA: Libraries Unlimited. Copyright © 2014.

Controlling Ads

- Facebook is supported by ads, so you'll always see them. The settings on this page let you determine how your information is used for ads, as well as the type of ads you see (to some extent.)
- **Third Party Sites** is where you can turn off the ability for Facebook to provide your information to third-party vendors so that they can use it for ads. Facebook does not currently do this, but according to its terms and conditions, it could do so at any time. To decline permission for Facebook to do this, click **Edit**. Look for **If we allow this in the future, show my information to**. In the drop-down box, choose **No one**. Click **Save Changes**.
- **Ads and Friends** deals with what your friends see in their ads based on your information. If I had this setting turned on, I could reasonably expect that my liking a store that sells cat products might lead to ads for kitty litter or collars on the pages of my friends. This happens because Facebook figures that you share interests with your friends, so it advertises according to your interests. To turn this setting off, click **Edit**. Look for **Pair my social actions with ads for**. Use the drop-down menu to choose **No one**. When you're done, click **Save Changes**.
- **Website and Mobile App Custom Audiences** controls cookies (or packets of information that a website stores about you to customize your experience on their page). These can be sent to Facebook from partnering sites for advertising purposes. To turn these off, look for **Opt out** in blue. It's a tiny link located under **Learn more**. The next page has lots of information on this. To turn it off, look for the **Opt out button** located in the middle of the page. Know that if you use multiple browsers (Firefox, Internet Explorer, etc.) and different computers to access Facebook, you'll need to repeat this on each since the setting works only within the browser you are currently using. A popup box will appear asking you if you'd like to opt out. Click **Submit** to save the setting. If you clear your cookies on a particular browser, you will need to opt out again.

Payments

- **Payments** lets you determine how you'd like to pay for in-app purchases, gift cards, and more if you choose to do so.

Support Dashboard

- If you're having technical problems with Facebook, check out **Support Dashboard** to see the status of any problems you've reported.

Additional Settings

- Now return to the arrow at the upper right-hand corner of the page.
- Under **Settings**, you'll see the link to **Log Out**. If you share a computer, you should always log out when you're finished with your Facebook session.
- Next, you'll see the option for **Help**. Clicking this takes you to a support page with searchable questions and answers. If this doesn't solve your problem, use the final link under the arrow, **Report a Problem**.

CHAPTER 6

LinkedIn

LinkedIn is a social media website that connects professionals around the world for purposes of networking, sharing ideas, recruiting, and job searching. It's a massive social network at well over 259 million, and is one of the oldest and most respected, too.

HOW TO PREPARE

If you haven't used your account in a while, now is a great time to sign in and update! LinkedIn has made lots of changes in the past few years. Update your profile, add some members to your networks, subscribe to Pulse to get news and updates from your field, and check out the greatly simplified privacy and security controls. Learning how to use LinkedIn isn't especially difficult since it's fairly intuitive.

Once you are up to date on the way everything works within LinkedIn, you may want to do some reading on ways to use LinkedIn as a part of a networking and job hunting strategy. There's no end of articles on this topic (try Mashable or *Wired*, as well as within LinkedIn itself). Most libraries carry a variety of books on LinkedIn strategy, too, which can be very useful. There's no need to read a whole book, unless you want to; just browse the contents or index to pull out some tips and tricks for your students. Acquaint yourself with the basics so that you can answer some strategy questions. If this is beyond the scope of your class or beyond your expertise, consider bringing in an expert.

COMMON QUESTIONS AND CONCERNS

As with many of the classes you teach for the public, the disparity of skill sets will be your biggest hurdle here. Some people will have no account, while others will have used the site extensively and have done a great deal of research on tips and strategies for maximizing their accounts. Thankfully, there are some things you can do to mitigate potential problems.

The first way to help your students is to write a very clear class description. If you're going to cover basics and your class is only for absolute beginners, say so explicitly. You may want to consider offering two different classes. The first can be for those just starting out, while the second can be for those who have mastered the basics and now want to learn about strategy. Consider asking an area expert to be available for one-on-one help after your session, too.

POSSIBLE VARIATIONS

There are many types of LinkedIn classes out there; so before designing your class, it's wise to do a little research to see what's already being offered in your community, and what might be needed. Beside your garden-variety basics class, you can teach classes on strategies, profile building, LinkedIn Etiquette, LinkedIn for Networking, LinkedIn for Job Searchers, LinkedIn for New Professionals, LinkedIn for Businesses and Hiring Managers, and lots more. You might even consider teaching a LinkedIn for Seniors class. The service can be great for finding volunteer opportunities, staying up to date with interesting information, networking, and consulting. Consider partnering with your local senior center for something like this. Finally, consider providing drop-in sessions for their specific questions.

SPECIAL CONSIDERATIONS

The list of potential community partners for a class like this is virtually endless. Consider working with your local senior center, career or placement center, recruiters, or even your local school district. Any of these groups can act as either a consultant or a partner. You could create a series of classes, each focusing on a different aspect of LinkedIn with a different group. You might want to offer drop-in sessions with an expert, too. Patrons love these since they provide one-on-one answers to their questions. Maybe you could consider LinkedIn as part of area job fairs, too. There are many ways to spin this class so that it works for your specific audience.

INSTRUCTOR NOTES

Logistics

The class below is for LinkedIn basics. This should help your students navigate LinkedIn and help them understand how it works. For this class, expect to spend about 45 minutes teaching. The handout below (and the class) can be tailored in any number of ways, as detailed above.

Consider creating a short bibliography of a few very current articles on LinkedIn strategy. You can add those to the end of the handout. You might also display your most current books on LinkedIn for students to check out.

What Is LinkedIn?

- LinkedIn is a social networking tool that helps you connect with professionals in your field. There are millions of users of LinkedIn, making it a valuable tool for increasing visibility and making connections in your field. In fact, many employers routinely check LinkedIn when hiring. You might think of it as Facebook for your professional life.
- In this class, you'll set up your new LinkedIn account, make some connections, and explore basic techniques that will help to get you started.

How Do I Get Started?

- To begin, go to www.linkedin.com. On the right side of the page, there is a box that says **Join LinkedIn Today**. Fill out the form in the box completely and click the green **Join Now** button.
- The next page will help you create your profile. Be as clear and accurate as possible, since this is information your colleagues and potential employers will see. For best results, treat it as you would a resume. Enter the information requested, and click **Enter LinkedIn**.
- Now take a moment to check your email. There should be a message from LinkedIn confirming your account. Click the first link in the email to verify that your email address is correct. A box will pop up asking you to confirm your email. Click **Confirm**, then type in the password that you chose for your LinkedIn account. Click **Sign In**. Your account is now confirmed, and you're ready to start adding content to your profile.

Adding Content to Your Profile

- Your profile page is possibly the most important part of your LinkedIn presence. You want to be as complete as possible since this can act as your resume for many prospective employers.
- To navigate to your profile page, mouse over **Profile**. A drop-down menu will appear. Click **Edit Profile**. You'll have many options on this page. Let's start in the left column.

- First, you'll see an area where you can **Add a Photo**. Click this to upload a photo from your computer. This process is nearly identical to attaching a document to your email. Just click **Browse** and select the file you'd like to use. Then click **Upload Photo**. You'll want this photo to be of you, and to be a professional image that's appropriate for hiring managers and other professionals to see. It's really important to have a photo here—you want potential employers and business contacts to be able to put a face to the name they see.
- When you're done, click **Edit Profile** again to return to your profile page.
- You may wish to edit your name to reflect your maiden and married name. Just click the pencil next to your name to do this.
- Below your name, you'll see your **Professional Headline**, which is essentially your job description and your workplace. Click on the link provided for more examples of what you might write here. When you're finished, click **Save**.
- To add or change your location and industry, just look below your professional headline. To change or add any of this information, just click the pencil, update the information, and click **Save**.
- Underneath your location and industry information and to the right, you'll see how many connections you have. More on connections later.

Viewing Your Public Profile

- Directly under your profile picture, you'll see a URL. Click **Edit** next to this to see how your profile appears to the public.
- The left side of this public profile page lists your basic information. The right side lets you **Customize Your Public Profile**. This option allows you to specify whether you'd like your public profile to be visible to everyone who searches for you, or no one. You'll also be able to choose which parts of your profile are visible by checking the boxes next to each.
- If you'd like to customize your public profile URL, you can do that under the Customize Your Public Profile section. Just click the link and type in the new. When you're done, click **Set Custom URL**.
- **Profile Badges** creates an embeddable link to your profile. This is a terrific way to connect to blogs, resumes, or any other online presence you have.
- Mouse over **Profile** and select **Edit Profile** to return to our editing page.

Background

- The next section is **Background**. This is a great place to update your background and include samples of your work.

- Click +**Add a Summary** to write a quick professional blurb about yourself. Be sure to spell check this carefully, as it will be visible to those who view your profile. When you're done, click **Save**.
- If you'd like to upload documents, photos, or video, you can do this right below.

Experience

- Next, you can +**Add a position** under **Experience**. Make sure you update this section any time you change jobs, since it helps potential new connections find you.
- Below +**Add a position**, you'll see your work history. You can add photos or other media to each position by clicking the little box icon with the plus sign in each section.
- If you need to change any elements of your work history, you can do so by clicking **Edit** next to the pencil icon located next to each job title. When you're finished, just click **Save**. If you need to, you can always delete an entry by clicking **Remove this position**.

Skills and Expertise

- Next, check out **Skills and Expertise**. These are endorsements that you've received from other people. Endorsements are a way for others to recommend you for particular skills and jobs without writing out a full recommendation.
- To add or remove endorsements, just click **Edit**, then **Add & Remove**. You also have the ability to choose whether you would like to display your endorsements by clicking **Display your endorsements?** You probably won't want to remove endorsements or choose not to display them unless they're completely wrong. Endorsements are great to have on your profile!

Education

- As you might expect, this section lets you edit and add your education. Don't forget to add practicums, in-service training, and internships, too.
- Add media (photos, links, video) to your education section, just as you did with your other profile information.

Additional Info

- In this section you can comment on or detail your interests, personal details, and contact information.

Connections

- To control whether you will allow others to see who you are connected with or keep that information private, click on **Customize visibility** under **Connections**.
- When requested, type in your password, then use the drop-down menu to make your selection. Click **Save Changes** when finished.
- Return to **Edit Profile** under **Profile**.

Groups

- Click the pencil next to **Groups** to view those that are currently associated with your profile.
- You can change the visibility for each group by clicking **Visible** under each.
- This is also the best place to leave a group or change the way that they contact you.
- A good rule of thumb is that it's helpful to be part of and active within at least three groups. This helps to show that you're engaged in your profession and its associations.

Following

- This section helps you to follow companies, which can be very useful if you're interested in possibly working for a particular company.
- To follow a company, just click the gold **Follow** button on the top of the company's LinkedIn page. You can follow up to 1,000 companies in this way.

Completing Your Profile

- Back at the top of your profile page, look for **Recommended for you**. This identifies items missing in your profile. Click into each of them and provide more information as you see fit.
- You may also choose to add extra details such as languages, publications, organizations, and much more. Just click on the corresponding word to add these.

Who's Viewed Your Profile

- By now you've probably noticed that when you mouse over **Profile**, the first option is to **Edit Profile** and the second is **Who's Viewed Your Profile**. As you might guess, this shows you who has been searching for you or clicking on your profile. This is excellent information to have—especially if you're networking or looking for a job. You can even contact those who searched for you to follow up. Just click **Connect** or **Send InMail** next to the name to do so.

Connections

- Now mouse over the **Connections** tab at the top of the page. You'll see three options.
- **Keep in Touch** shows you your list of connections on LinkedIn. Mouse over each to message or tag the connection. Click the name if you'd like to see the full profile page. If you'd like to delete a connection, you can do so by mousing over the name, then clicking **More**, and then clicking **Remove connection**.
- **Add Connections** appears next in the drop-down menu. This uses your email accounts to find people you may know on LinkedIn.
- Finally, **Find Alumni** helps you locate other professionals who went to school with you.

Adding Connections

- Connections are a vital part of your LinkedIn page. It is often the connections of your connections that prove to be most important, just as in real-life networking.
- Start by clicking **Add Connections** at the top of the page. The page that appears allows you to search for colleagues and other people you may be interested in networking with. Use your email addresses to do this.
- Or, if you prefer, you can also use the search bar at the top of the screen to search for and add people one at a time.
- After being confirmed as connections, these people will be listed under your **Contacts**. This list of colleagues is then categorized by companies, locations, industries, and activity. Click the name of each person to see more information about their workplaces and contacts.

Find Alumni

- Mouse over **Networks** again to see the drop-down menu you've been working with. Click **Find Alumni** to search for people who went to school with you.
- At the top of this page you can change schools, years, and where your classmates now live. Matches to your search will appear below.

- If you see someone you'd like to add to your connections, click the +**Connect** button below their name. You'll have the option to write a message to that person, then you can click the blue button that says **Send Invitation.**
- Sometimes LinkedIn may ask you how you know someone. You may have to specify which school you went to together, or where you were coworkers. If you don't have this information, LinkedIn will ask you to type in the email address of the content as a way to prove that you know them. This helps to keep connection requests limited to people you actually know.

A Note on Adding Connections

- LinkedIn characterizes potential contacts in a system of degrees. First-degree connections are people you know, and who you've already connected with. Second-degree connections are people who are connected with your connections (it's easiest to think of these as "mutual friends"). Third-degree connections are more distantly connected to you. They have a relationship with your second-degree connections.
- Your first-, second-, and third-degree connections are all considered part of your professional network. If your connection is more distant or you have no connection at all, the person will be considered out of your network. You can contact these people through LinkedIn mail, or InMail.

Jobs

- LinkedIn is a terrific place to look for a new job. There's a solid variety of jobs posted here without all the junk that often clutters up other job search sites.
- Start by clicking **Jobs**, found to the right of **Connections.**
- At the top of the page, you'll see an option to search for jobs. Just type in your profession in the box next to **Search** for a list of what's currently posted.
- Inside each job listing, you have the ability to save it for later or apply. You'll see information about the job and the company as well as a list of similar companies that are now hiring. You can also see which of your connections work there. If you have questions, you can contact the person who posted the job with an InMail.

Interests

- Now mouse over **Interests**, located to the right of **Jobs.**
- First, click on **Companies.** On this page, you can use the tabs to search for companies you'd like to follow and see the ones that you

already are following. You can stop following any of these companies at any time by clicking **Following** below the company.

- Now mouse over **Interests** again, and click on **Groups**. This shows
you groups that you are currently in. Click on any of these to see
what's new with the group. You will also see a list of **Groups you
may be interested in.**
- Next, under **Interests**, you'll see **Pulse**. This is an easy way to subscribe to channels of information and articles that might be of interest to you. Just click the + (plus sign) button over each to add these.
When you're ready to continue, click the **Next** button to continue.
The next page gives you a list of influencers. If you want to read
more by them, just click the + button over their pictures. When
you're finished, click **See Your News**. This page of updating stories
can always be accessed under **Pulse**.
- Mouse over **Interests** again to select the final option, **Education**. This
provides lots of information about your schools, including news and
links to find more connections.

Account Navigation Bar

- Now take a look at the top bar. This includes the search feature as
well as lots of your account information and navigation.
- On the far left side, you'll see the LinkedIn logo, a blue box that says
in. Click on this any time to get back to your main LinkedIn page.
- Now look for the search bar. You can use this to look for people,
companies, and a lot more. Just type in your search and click the
magnifying glass to see results. If you'd like to narrow your search,
use the gray box to the left of the search bar to restrict your results.
- **Advanced** gives you many great options to find members of groups,
schools, and other items of interest.
- The right side of the bar contains a few useful icons.
  - If you have notifications, a red number appears over the icon.
  - The envelope icon shows you connection requests as well as messages.
  - If you'd like to write a new message, just click the pencil and paper
    icon in the upper right-hand corner of that section. Otherwise,
    you can read and respond to any new message by clicking on it.
- The flag icon to the right of the envelope is for your general notifica-
tions. This includes endorsements, new connections, and profile views.
- The icon of the person and a plus sign is a shortcut to add connec-
tions.
- The final icon to the far right side is a square with your profile picture. Most of these settings are found elsewhere in LinkedIn, so for
now, just take a few minutes to go over the basics.

Profile and Account Settings

- When you mouse over your profile picture, you'll see a number of options for enhancing and editing your profile and adjusting your settings.
- The first option lists your name. This is another quick link to view and edit your profile. Next to your name, you should see a button to **Sign Out**. You should always use this when you are finished using LinkedIn.
- The second option tells you what type of account type you have. If you'd like, you can click **Upgrade** for pricing or account options. Most people use the free account, but these enhanced accounts can be helpful for job seekers and businesses.
- **Job Posting** and **Company Pages** are both helpful if you are using LinkedIn on behalf of your company.
- **Language** lets you change the language you access LinkedIn with.
- Now click on **Privacy & Settings**. You'll be asked to enter your password to access this page.

Privacy and Settings

- Notice your basic information in the light blue box at the top of your **Privacy & Settings** page. This is a great place to change your email and your password and upgrade your account, if you choose to do so.
- The bottom half of the page helps you navigate your settings. Use the tabs on the left side of the screen to move between settings.
- The **Profile** settings link asks you to update your preferences based on a series of questions. These are fairly clear and easy to use. To edit each setting, just click on the link.
- **Communications** lets you determine how often LinkedIn may contact you, and for what purposes.
- **Groups, Companies & Applications** allows you to set communication preferences for your groups and lets you control information that applications use.
- **Account** is a collection of links to settings found elsewhere with the exception of the **Close your account** link.

Help Center

- The last link under **Account & Settings** is **Help Center**. This is an awesome resource that you should use frequently! Here you'll find the answers to any of your questions, as well as tips and pointers on how to use LinkedIn more effectively.
- Don't see your question listed? Ask by clicking **Get Help**.

Closing

That's it! That's all there is to using LinkedIn. Now that you know the basics, you can begin using LinkedIn to start building your network. For more on using LinkedIn as effectively as possible, use the Help Center as well as the many articles online. If you'd like more in-depth information, try checking out one of the many books on LinkedIn strategy available at the library.

LINKEDIN ESSENTIALS

What Is LinkedIn?

- LinkedIn is a social networking tool that helps you connect with professionals in your field. This handout explains how to set up your new LinkedIn account, make some connections, and explore other basics that will help to get you started.

How Do I Get Started?

- To begin, go to www.linkedin.com. On the right side of the page, there is a box that says **Join LinkedIn Today**. Fill out the form in the box completely and click the green **Join Now** button. Answer the short questionnaire, then click **Enter LinkedIn**. Now take a moment to check your email to confirm your account.

Adding Content to Your Profile

- To navigate to your profile page, mouse over **Profile**. A drop-down menu will appear. Click **Edit Profile**. You'll find many options on this page that can help you update your profile. You'll want to have a recent photo to upload as well as the most complete job history and industry information possible. Take a few minutes to update this information now.

Update Your Background

- This is a great place to update your background and include samples of your work.
- Click +**Add a Summary** to write a quick professional blurb about yourself.
- If you'd like to upload documents, photos, or video, you can do this right below.

Add Experience

- Next, you can +**Add a position** under **Experience**. Make sure you update this section any time you change jobs, since it helps potential new connections find you.
- Below +**Add a position**, you'll see your work history. Take a few moments to add photos or other media to this section.
- If you need to change any elements of your work history, you can do so by clicking **Edit** next to the pencil icon located next to each job title. When you're finished, click **Save**. If you need to delete an entry, you can always click **Remove this position**.

Skills and Expertise

- This section collects endorsements that you've received from other people. Endorsements are a way for others to recommend you for particular skills and jobs without writing out a full recommendation.

From *Teaching Social Media: The Can-Do Guide* by Liz Kirchhoff.
Santa Barbara, CA: Libraries Unlimited. Copyright © 2014.

- To add or remove endorsements just click **Edit**, then **Add & Remove**. You also can choose whether you would like to display your endorsements by clicking **Display your endorsements?**

Education

- As you might expect, this section lets you edit and add your education. Don't forget to add practicums, in-service trainings, and internships. You may also add media to this section.

Additional Info

- In this section you can comment on your interests, personal details, and contact information.

Connections

- Click on **Customize visibility** under **Connections** to decide whether you will allow others to see who you are connected with or keep that information private.
- When requested, type in your password, then use the drop-down menu to make your selection. Click **Save Changes** when finished.
- Return to **Edit Profile** under **Profile**.

Groups

- Click the pencil next to **Groups** to view those that are currently associated with your profile. You may also leave a group or change the way that they contact you.
- Try to be active within at least three groups. This helps to show that you're engaged in your profession and its associations.

Following

- This section helps you to follow companies. If you're interested in possibly working for a particular company, this feature can be very useful.
- To follow a company, just click the gold **Follow** button on the top of their LinkedIn page. You can follow up to a thousand companies in this way.

Completing Your Profile

- Back at the top of your profile page, you'll see a link that says **Recommended for you**. This lists items missing in your profile. Click into each of them to provide more information.

Who's Viewed Your Profile

- By now you've probably noticed that when you mouse over **Profile**, the first option is to **Edit Profile** and the second is **Who's Viewed Your Profile**. If you're networking or looking for a job, you can contact those who searched for you to follow up. Just click **Connect** or **Send InMail** next to the name to do so.

(continued)

Connections

- Now mouse over the **Connections** tab at the top of the page. You'll see three options.
- **Keep in Touch** shows you your list of connections on LinkedIn. Mouse over each to message or tag the connection. Click the name if you'd like to see the full profile page. If you'd like to delete a connection, you can do so by mousing over the name, clicking **More**, then clicking **Remove connection**.
- **Add Connections** appears next in the drop-down menu. This uses your email accounts to find people you may know on LinkedIn.
- Finally, **Find Alumni** helps you locate other professionals who went to school with you.

Adding Connections

- Connections are a vital part of your LinkedIn page. It is often the connections of your connections that prove to be most important, just as in real-life networking.
- Start by clicking **Add Connections** at the top of the page. The page that appears allows you to search for colleagues and other people you may be interested in networking with. You'll use your email addresses to do this.
- If you prefer, you can use the search bar at the top of the screen to search for and add people one at a time.
- After being confirmed, these people will be listed under Contacts. This list of colleagues is then categorized by companies, locations, industries, and activity. Click the name of each person to see more information about their workplaces and contacts.

Find Alumni

- Mouse over **Connections** again to see the drop-down menu we've been working with. Click **Find Alumni** to search for people who went to school with you.
- At the top of this page, you can change schools, years, and where your classmates now live. Matches to your search will appear below.
- If you see someone you'd like to add to your connections, click the +**Connect** button below their name. You'll have the option to write a message, then you can click the blue button that says **Send Invitation**. You may need to specify how you know the person before you can add them.

Jobs

- LinkedIn is a terrific place to look for a new job. There's a solid variety of jobs posted here without all the junk that often clutters up other job search sites.
- Start by clicking **Jobs**, found to the right of **Connections**.
- At the top of the page, you'll see an option to search for jobs. Just type in your profession in the box next to **Search** for a list of what's currently posted.

From *Teaching Social Media: The Can-Do Guide* by Liz Kirchhoff.
Santa Barbara, CA: Libraries Unlimited. Copyright © 2014.

- Inside each job listing, you have the ability to save it for later or apply. You'll see information about the job and the company as well as a list of similar companies that are now hiring. You can also see which of your connections work there. If you have questions, you can contact the person who posted the job with an InMail.

Interests

- Now mouse over **Interests**, located to the right of **Jobs**.
- Click on **Companies** to find and follow those you are interested in. You can also follow **Groups** or find more contacts in **Education**.
- Next, under **Interests**, you'll see **Pulse**. This is an easy way to subscribe to channels of information and articles that might be of interest to you. Just click the "+" over each to add these. When you're ready to continue, click the **Next** button to continue. The next page gives you a list of influencers. If you want to read more by them, just click the + over their pictures. When you're finished, click **See Your News**. This page of updating stories can always be accessed under **Pulse**.

Account Navigation Bar

- Now take a look at the top bar. This includes the search feature as well as lots of your account information and navigation.
- On the far left side, you'll see the LinkedIn logo, a blue box that says **in**. Click on this any time to get back to your main LinkedIn page.
- Next, you'll see a search bar. Just type in your search and click the magnifying glass to see results. Use the gray box to the left of the search bar to restrict your results.
- **Advanced** gives you tons of great options to find members of groups, schools, and other individuals of interest.
- The right side of the bar has a few useful icons.
  - If you have notifications, a red number appears over the icon.
  - The envelope icon shows you connection requests as well as messages.
  - If you'd like to write a new message, just click the pencil and paper icon in the upper right-hand corner of that section. Otherwise, you can read and respond to any new message by clicking on it.
- The flag icon to the right of the envelope tracks your general notifications. This includes endorsements, new connections, and profile views.
- The icon of the person and a plus sign is a shortcut to add connections.
- The final icon to the far right side is a square with your profile picture. Most of these settings are elsewhere in LinkedIn, so for now, just take a few minutes to go over the basics.

Profile and Account Settings

- When you mouse over your profile picture, you'll see a number of options for enhancing and editing your profile and adjusting your settings.

(continued)

- The first option lists your name. This is another quick link to view and edit your profile. Next to your name, you should see a button to **Sign Out**. Like all social media, it's important to sign out to avoid unauthorized use of your account. It's especially important on LinkedIn because this is a forum where you are being evaluated based partially on your professionalism.
- The second option tells you what type of account you have. If you'd like, you can click **Upgrade** for pricing or account options. Most people use the free account, but these enhanced accounts can be helpful for job seekers and businesses who wish to see more detailed information.
- **Job Posting** and **Company Pages** are both helpful if you are using LinkedIn on behalf of your company.
- **Language** lets you change the language you access LinkedIn with.

Privacy and Settings

- Now click on **Privacy & Settings**. You'll be asked to enter your password to access this page.
- Your basic information appears in the light blue box at the top of your **Privacy & Settings** page. This is a good place to change your email and your password, as well as to upgrade your account, if you choose to do so.
- The bottom half of the page helps you navigate your settings. Use the tabs on the left side of the screen to move between settings.

Help Center

- The last link under **Account & Settings** is **Help Center**. This is an awesome resource that you should use frequently! Here you'll find the answers to any of your questions, as well as tips and pointers on how to use LinkedIn more effectively.
- Don't see your question listed? Ask by clicking **Get Help**.

Terms

- **Connections:** The people who make up your LinkedIn network.
- **First-degree connections:** People you personally know. These can be coworkers and friends.
- **Second-degree connection:** Connections of the people in your network.
- **Third-degree connection:** Connections of your second-degree connections.
- **InMail:** LinkedIn email.
- **Pulse:** News and articles tailored to your interests and profession.
- **Endorsements:** Recommendations by your connections that recognize your skills and assets.

Resources

- **Mashable LinkedIn Guide:** http://mashable.com/category/linkedin/
- **LinkedIn Help Center:** http://help.linkedin.com/app/home

From *Teaching Social Media: The Can-Do Guide* by Liz Kirchhoff.
Santa Barbara, CA: Libraries Unlimited. Copyright © 2014.

CHAPTER 7

Google+

Google+ is an interesting and easy-to-use social network that combines many aspects of other online services. While it is probably used less than some of the other social networking sites, it is often more visible, since it works with the Internet giant Google.

Google+ can be used for most social networking functions. Users organize friends into "circles," or groups of people who can all see the same content. This makes sharing fast and easy, but also more targeted than it is in other social networking sites. Because Google is such a force in the Internet world, opportunities to share to it are more pervasive than other services.

HOW TO PREPARE

Lots of people created Google+ accounts when the service first opened for business. Because the service was brand new and there wasn't much content, many people never went back. If this describes you, it's time! Go back into your account and give things another test run. Add more friends to your circles, and follow more pages. Play with the security settings, upload some photos, and use the +1 feature. Take a few minutes to try a Hangout, too. If you don't have an account, set one up. You can use any existing Google account to open your Google+ account.

COMMON QUESTIONS AND CONCERNS

Privacy is probably the biggest concern that will be raised in your class. Many people find it unsettling that Google has so much information about the average user. Google+ does use this information. For example, Google+ uses your search history with Google to recommend places to review. If you have a Gmail account, Google+ will recommend that you become friends with some of the people you email. YouTube is owned by Google and requires a Google+ account to comment. Overall, it's hard to avoid exposing your information to Google, because so many of these accounts are tied together. Students can get around some of this by logging out of their account before searching. However, if any of your students are really unnerved by this, you can tell them to simply observe, and consider the class a demonstration.

On the flip side, many of your students will probably already use Google+ for business or networking, or for keeping up with trends in their field. It's possible that many people probably won't care much about whether or how their information is being used, because Google won't have much deep or meaningful information about them anyway.

POSSIBLE CLASS VARIATIONS

This class could easily be taught with a business focus. Google+ is a great way to follow workplace and industry trends, networks, and other areas of interest. You could also teach an abbreviated version of Google+ with LinkedIn, since because of their professional focus and applications, they go together in so many ways.

Since Google+ is highly visual and even beautiful, you might also consider teaching it as a class for artists, crafters, and patrons who like creating video. Google+ can be a terrific place to showcase and promote creativity.

INSTRUCTOR NOTES

Logistics

Google+ can either be taught in a full class of 45 minutes to an hour, or shortened to work with other classes that you'd like to pair it with. Try to leave at least 15 minutes for questions, as there is often a bit of discussion about Google+ versus other social networking, as well as privacy.

Getting Started

- Sign into Google with any Google account. Just go to www .google.com and click in the upper right-hand corner to sign in. Your Gmail account works for this! If you don't already have an account, follow the prompts to set one up.
- Look on the right side of the page. Notice the icon that looks like four squares. Click on this, and look for the red **g+**. Click this to get to Google+.

Setting Up Your Account and Finding Friends

- The first page you see shows you a list of people you may know. If you use Gmail or other Google services, Google collects and uses that information to populate this list.
- Add friends by clicking **Add** next to each name. Check the box next to your relationship with the person. This helps Google+ add people to appropriate circles. When you're all done, click the blue button that says **Continue on to Google+**.

Your Google+ Home Page

- Now your account is set up, and you'll be redirected to your Google+ home page. We'll start in the menu on the left side of the page and work our way around the site.
- Start by clicking the **Home** button. You'll see a menu of options to help you navigate Google+.

Profile

- The first option under **Home** is **Profile**. Clicking this takes you to the page that others see when they search for you. Here you'll see your circles, past posts, and more. You can change your profile picture and cover picture here as well.
- Now take a moment to consider enhancing your profile. To add a profile picture, just mouse over the circle with the person icon. An image of a camera will appear. When you click on it, you'll be able to upload a picture. Just select the appropriate file from your computer. Once the picture is in Google, use the provided squares to drag and crop the image. When you're done, click **Set as profile photo**.
- If you'd like, you can now **Post about your new photo**. This will be a popup box that will display the photo you just uploaded. You can add a comment above the image, and type in the names, emails, or circles of those whom you wish to see the update below. When you're done, click **Share**.
- You may want to change the cover picture, or wallpaper of your profile. To do this, just mouse over the cover picture until you see **Change cover**. Click this. Google+ has a gallery of cover images, or you can use the tabs on the top of the page to upload or search for your own. Once you've picked one, click it to select it, then click the blue **Select cover photo** in the bottom left-hand corner.
- Now look below your profile picture and cover photo. You should see a number of tabs.

- **About** lets you share lots of background information about yourself. If you'd like to add in details about your education, hometown, and workplace, this is the best place for that information. To change any of these, just click the blue **Edit** button in each section.
- **Posts** displays your posting history and tells you who you've shared each with. This is a great place to edit or remove posts. Just look for the downward arrow in each. Just follow the prompts to edit, delete, disable comments, and disable reshares.
- **Photos** displays all the pictures you've uploaded. Click into a photo to see how it is shared and to use the basic photo editing tools.
- **Videos** lets you view or delete any videos you've uploaded to Google+.
- **+1's** are things that you've liked online. When you click this icon on websites around the Internet, you'll be saving the links to this page. These are great as recommendations, or to note websites and articles you'd like to access later.
- **Reviews** works a lot like Yelp. You just use Google+ to check in and rate a business.
- Now let's return to your menu options in the upper left-hand corner by mousing over **Profile** to check out another feature of Google+.

People

- Now click **People**. **People** is a great way to find and add users you know.
- The middle of the page has a number of suggestions of people Google thinks you might know based on mutual friends and classmates. Recognize someone? Click **Add** under their name. Google will ask you to specify which circle you'd like to add them to. Check the appropriate box, or click **Create new circle** if none of them quite fit.
- In the menu on the left side of the screen, click **Search for anyone** to find friends by school, city, company, or email.
- Click **Added you** to see who has added you and reciprocate.
- **Gmail contacts** uses your email contacts to find more friends.
- **Find coworkers** helps you find current and former coworkers. This can be really helpful for networking.
- **Find classmates** prompts you to fill in your school information to generate a list of people who attended with you. Add multiple schools by clicking this button again.
- Finally, **Connect services** lets you search other email accounts for contacts you might wish to add to Google+.
- Now that you know how to add friends, return to the menu on the top left-hand side of the screen.

Photos

- Click **People** to see the full menu, then click **Photos**. This page will help you organize and upload photos to share with your circles.
- The default for this page is **Highlights**. You can also view pictures by **Albums** by clicking the link at the top of the page.
- Under **More**, you can **Backup** (or save photos), see **Photos of you**, **Trash**, or **Take a tour**.
- Next to **More**, you can **Upload photos**.
- To upload, either drag and drop photos into Google+ or **Click to open file browser** to upload the same way as you would attach a file to email.
- Once you've uploaded an item, you'll be able to **Add to album**, change the view, and organize photos by **Date taken, Name,** and **Reverse**. You can find these last three options under the downward arrow in the upper right-hand corner.
- When you're finished, click **Done**—the blue button in the bottom left-hand corner of the screen.
- Back on your main Photos page, check the right side of the screen for additional options.
- **Share** lets you send your photo to the circle or individual people you specify.
- **Tag people** helps you specify who was with you in the photo.
- The downward arrow to the far right has a number of organizing and sharing options.
- **Add photos** is another place to upload pictures.
- **Sharing options** allows you to edit your album name and who you share it with. The bottom of the page also has a link that you can use to send your photos or album to others. Click **Save** when you are finished working with this page.
- The next option under the arrow is **Download album**. This option makes Google+ a really handy place to store your photos online.
- **Add to event** allows you to add your pictures to a group or event page. This option is available to all guests of the event. Your pictures will also be viewable by everyone.
- **Move album to trash** deletes the album.
- **Apply Auto Enhance** provides three levels of color correction to selected photos.
- **Hide from highlights** removes the selected picture or album from the highlights area of your profile.
- Keep in mind that you can apply all of these options to particular photos as well as to the entire album. Just click any photo to select it. Once you select the images, you'll see a blue bar at the top of the page with the same types of options.

- Now click **Photos** in the left-hand corner to get back to the main menu.

What's Hot

- Click **What's hot. What's hot** shows you a selection of the most popular content on Google+. These can be posts, videos, GIFs, links, and more. These are determined from searches over the entire web, rather than from people in your circles.
- Look for **Trending**, which lists the most discussed topics on Google+ at the moment. Click a word to see public related posts. This is a great discovery tool!
- **Communities you might like** recommends groups based on your interests and what your friends like.
- **Interesting people and pages** gives recommendations based on categories.
- **You might like** helps you follow pages for services and groups.
- Mouse over any post in the **What's hot** category to get a downward arrow in the right corner. Click on this to see a menu that gives you the options to share, embed, mute, or report the post. The final option in the menu, **View Ripples**, shows the number of public shares the post has had. If you'd like to follow the person who posted the content, just mouse over their name and click **Follow**. You'll be asked to select a circle. **Following** tends to work well for this type of thing, but categorize as you'd like.
- Return to the main menu by clicking **What's hot** in the upper left-hand menu.

Communities

- Click **Communities. Communities** is sorted into two categories at the top of the page. The first, **All communities,** includes everything on Google+. The second, **Recommended for you,** makes suggestions based on what you like. The longer you're on Google+ and the more information the service has about you, the better these recommendations will be.
- Click the name of a community to see the page. If you'd like to join the community, just click the red **Join community** in the upper right-hand corner of the page.
- If you ultimately decide the community isn't for you, just look for the gear symbol on the left side of the page. Click the icon, and choose **Leave community.** You can also use this menu to determine how many posts you'd like to see in your Home stream.

- Click **Recommended for you** at the top of the page to return to the previous page.
- To find communities that you're interested in, just click the white box that says **Search for communities**. You'll find this in the upper right-hand corner of the main Communities page.
- You can click on **Create community** if you don't find anything appealing to you.
- Click **Communities** in the upper left-hand corner to return to the main menu.

Events

- Now click **Events**. **Events** allows you to set up a gathering, or a cause-based group, create invitations, and track RSVPs. You can share photos with the entire group of invited people, post your photo stream while at the event, and see the event on your Google Calendar.
- Click **Create event** to get started.
- Want to view scheduled events? Just use the tabs at the top of the page to navigate to **Find more events**.
- Click **Events** in the upper left-hand corner to return to the main menu.

Hangouts

- Now click **Hangouts**. **Hangouts** is a fun, easy way to video- and voice-chat with your friends. You can use it with one person, or talk with up to 10 people at one time. Computer-to-phone calls are free within the United States and Canada.
- You can use Hangouts on multiple pages within Google+ or even from your Gmail account.
- If you like, try **Hangouts on Air**. These are hangout sessions that are live streamed. When the event is done, the video is posted on Google+ and your YouTube channel. Click **Start a Hangout On Air** to start this.
- Want to try a regular hangout? Look for the Hangout sidebar on the right side of the page. Click **Enable my circles** to get started. Now click **+New Hangout**. You'll see a box after the name of each person. As you check boxes, the names of the people you select appear at the top of the screen. Click the text icon to write a message, or the video icon to video chat.
- Want to talk to a group? Click **Start a video party**. If you've been invited to participate in a Hangout, that will appear under the tab at the top of the page that says **Video parties**.

- Click **Hangouts** in the upper left-hand corner to return to the main menu.

Pages

- Now click **Pages**. **Pages** are great for promoting and sharing information about businesses, causes, and products.
- Getting started is easy! Just click **Create a page**.
- Click **Pages** in the upper left-hand corner to return to the main menu.

Local

- Now click **Local**. **Local** is a review site that works like Yelp. If you'd like general suggestions, browse the middle of the page. Recommended businesses are listed by category (e.g., restaurants, dog groomers, etc.).
- Use the boxes at the top of the page to search for businesses in your area. Use the reviews and star ratings to make a more informed decision.
- Want to write a review? Search for the location first. The business listing will have a pencil icon in the upper right-hand corner. Click this to write your review and set your star rating.
- Click **Local** in the upper left-hand corner to return to the main menu.

Settings

- Now click **Settings**. First, we'll discuss **Google+ Settings**. This should be the defaulted page when you click on **Settings**. If not, click on **Google+** on the left side of the page.
- This page asks a series of questions to help you control your privacy.
- Start with **Who can interact with you and your posts. Who can send you notifications?** lets you choose how often you get notified about something.
  - ○ **Anyone** means that you will get notified anytime anyone posts anything.
  - ○ **Only you** restricts these notifications, so that you see only your own content.
  - ○ Or if you prefer, choose **Custom**, which lets you decide which people you will see notifications from. You can view your notifications any time by clicking on the bell in the upper right-hand corner of the page.

- ○ **Who can comment on your public posts?** lets you determine who can comment on your freely available things. The options are essentially the same as above, from **Anyone** down to **Only you** or **Custom.**
- **Who can Hangout with you** lets you decide who you'd like to accept Hangout requests from. Click **Customize** to get a list of your circles. You'll be able to use the drop-down menus to adjust each circle. Getting too many notifications? Uncheck the box that says **Get notified about Hangout requests.**
- **Shared Endorsements** allows businesses to use your reviews and recommendations in ads. If you would prefer to not allow this, click **Edit,** then scroll down the page until you see **Based on my activity, Google may show my name and profile photo in shared endorsements that appear in ads.** Uncheck the box and click **Save.** A popup box will appear to help you confirm. Click **Continue.** You can always return to this setting later to change it if you wish to do so.
- Click **Back to Account Settings** in the upper left-hand corner to return to the previous page.
- **Notification delivery** allows you to choose whether you'd like to be notified by phone or email. You can include additional phone numbers and email addresses here, too.
- **Manage subscriptions** has two boxes to check if you'd like to be updated on activity outside of your normal circles, or if you'd like Google+ news.
- **Receive notifications** lets you specify which updates you'd like to be notified about. By default, these are all checked. If you want to limit the updates and notifications you receive, just uncheck those you don't need updates about.
- **Google+ Pages** acts as a shortcut to add a page once you've searched Google with a "+" (plus sign) and a company name. Check the box if you'd like to add this feature.
- **Apps & activities** lets you manage any apps you use within Google. To use it, click **Manage apps & activities.** You probably won't have anything to manage yet, so you can return to this setting later.
- **Your circles** allows you to set the default for who automatically sees content that you share. Click **Customize** if you'd like to edit the Google+ default.
- **Accessibility** is a great option for people with visual impairment. It changes the layout of the page, so that it's easier to read. Check the box if you'd like to use this feature and customize page layout.
- The next section helps you manage your **Photos.** Check the box in front of each option you'd like to use. Note that this section also tells you how much storage space you've used. Google+ gives you 15 GB

of space. If you use that much and would like more, you may purchase it.

- **Google Drive**, formerly Google Docs, is a great place to store documents, slideshows, and photos. This next option allows you to check a box if you'd like Google+ to add those images to your library. This only makes them more easily available to you, and doesn't automatically share them.
- **Auto Enhance** provides color correction for your photos. Select the appropriate checkbox for how much you'd like Google+ to apply this tool.
- **Auto Awesome** combines your photos into animations or group pictures. This is on by default. If you'd like to turn it off, uncheck the box.
- Under **Auto Awesome**, you'll see an option to auto-approve tags by a particular group. When someone from this circle tags you, it will automatically appear on your profile. To change this, just click the X next to the name of the circle. If you'd like to add a circle or individuals to this setting, click +**Add more people**.
- **Profile** offers you a series of options to determine the visibility of some elements of your profile. Take a moment now to read through these and select those you'd like to activate.
- **Hashtags** automatically adds searchable words from Google to your posts. This helps make your posts easier to find.
- **Location Settings** should be currently unchecked. If you choose to turn this feature on, it will work a bit like Foursquare. Your places will then be visible to your circles.
- Finally, if you decide that Google+ isn't for you, you can delete your profile under **Disable Google+**.
- If you choose to do so, there are several more sets of privacy controls within Google. Because they aren't specifically for Google+, we won't cover them here; but if you would like to review them, look for their category listings on the left-hand side of the page.

Closing

Now you know the basics of your new Google+ account, and you can start adding content to your pages and connecting with lots of new people. If you have questions or would like additional help, feel free to contact us anytime.

GOOGLE+ ESSENTIALS

Getting Started

- Sign into Google with any Google account. Your Gmail account works for this!
- Look on the right side of the page. There's an icon that looks like four squares. Click on this, and look for the red **g+**. Click this to get to Google+.

Setting Up Your Account and Finding Friends

- The first page you should see will show you a list of people you may know. If you use Gmail or other Google services, Google uses those contacts to populate this list.
- Add friends by clicking **Add** next to each name. Check the box next to your relationship with the person. This helps Google+ add people to appropriate circles. When you're all done, click the blue button that says **Continue on to Google+**.

Profile

- Most of the navigation within your Google+ profile will take place on the left side of the screen. Click the name of the page that you're on to access the menu options.
- Click **Profile**.
- Use the options on this page to add a profile picture, change your cover image, and edit your profile. You'll also be able to view your posting history. This page also displays media such as photos and video, and organizes your +1s.

People

- **People** gives you a great way to find and add users you know to your circles.
- Browse the middle of the page to find people you know, and click **Add** under their name. Google will ask you to specify which circle you'd like to add them to. Check the appropriate box, or click **Create new circle** if none of them quite fit.
- In the menu on the left side of the screen, click **Search for anyone** to find friends by school, city, company, or email.
- Click **Added you** to see who has added you to their circles, and reciprocate if you'd like to add them to yours.
- **Gmail contacts** scans your Google email contacts to find more friends.
- **Find coworkers** helps you find current and former coworkers. This can be really helpful for networking.
- **Find classmates** prompts you to fill in your school information to generate a list of people who attended with you. Add multiple schools by clicking this button again.
- Finally, **Connect services** allows you to search other email accounts for contacts you might wish to add to Google+.

(continued)

From *Teaching Social Media: The Can-Do Guide* by Liz Kirchhoff.
Santa Barbara, CA: Libraries Unlimited. Copyright © 2014.

Photos

- This page helps you organize and upload photos.
- The default for this page is **Highlights**. You can also view pictures by **Albums** by clicking the link at the top of the page.
- Under **More**, you can **Backup**, see **Photos of you, Trash**, or **Take a tour**.
- Next to **More**, you can **Upload photos**.
- When uploading, you can either drag and drop photos into Google+ or **Click to open file browser** to upload the same way as you would attach a file to email.
- Once you've uploaded an item, you'll be able to **Add to album**, change the view, and organize photos by **Date taken, Name**, and **Reverse**. You can find these last three options under the downward arrow in the upper right-hand corner.
- When you're finished, click **Done**—the blue button in the bottom left-hand corner of the screen.
- Back on your main Photos page, look to the right side of the screen for additional options.
- **Share** lets you send your photo to the circle or individual people you specify.
- **Tag people** lets you specify who was with you in the photo.
- The downward arrow to the far right has a number of organizing and sharing options.
- **Add photos** gives you another place to upload pictures.
- **Sharing options** lets you edit your album name and who you share it with. Click **Save** when you are finished working with this page.
- The next option under the arrow is **Download album**. This option makes Google+ a really handy place to store your photos online.
- **Add to event** allows you to add your pictures to the page of a group or event. This option will be available to all guests of the event. Your pictures will also be viewable by everyone.
- **Move album to trash** deletes the album.
- **Apply Auto Enhance** provides three levels of color correction to selected photos.
- **Hide from highlights** removes the selected picture or album from the high-lights area of your profile.

What's Hot

- **What's hot** is a selection of the most popular content on Google+. These can be posts, videos, GIFs, links, and more.
- Look for **Trending**, the most discussed topics on Google+ at the moment.
- **Communities you might like** recommends groups based on your interests and what your friends like.
- **Interesting people and pages** gives recommendations based on categories.
- **You might like** lets you follow pages for services and groups.
- Mouse over any post in the **What's hot** category to get a downward arrow in the right corner. Click on this to see a menu that allows you to share, embed, mute, or report the post. The final option in the menu, **View Ripples**, shows the number of public shares the post has had. If you'd like to follow the

person who posted the content, just mouse over their name and click **Follow**. You'll be asked to select a circle. **Following** tends to work well for this type of thing, but categorize as you'd like.

Communities

- **Communities** is sorted into two categories at the top of the page. The first, **All communities**, includes everything on Google+. The second, **Recommended for you**, makes suggestions based on what you like.
- Click the name of a community to see the page. Join or leave the community at any time in the upper right-hand corner of the page.
- **Search for communities** to find other communities you might like.
- Click **Create community** if you don't find anything appealing to you.

Events

- **Events** allows you to set up a gathering or cause, create invitations, share pictures, and track RSVPs.
- Click **Create event** to get started or view scheduled events under **Find more events**.

Hangouts

- **Hangouts** is a fun, easy way to video- and voice-chat with your friends. You can use it with one person, or talk with up to 10 people at one time.
- If you'd like, you can try **Hangouts on Air**. These are hangouts that are live streamed. When the event is done, the video is posted on Google+ and your YouTube channel. Click **Start a Hangout On Air** to do this.
- Want to try a regular hangout? Look for the Hangout sidebar on the right side of the page. Click **Enable my circles** to get started. Now click **+New Hangout**. You'll see a box after the name of each person. As you check boxes, the names of the people you select will appear at the top of the screen. Click the text icon to write a message, or the video icon to video chat.
- Want to talk to a group? Click **Start a video party**. If you've been invited to participate in a Hangout, that will appear under the tab at the top of the page that says **Video parties**.

Pages

- **Pages** are great for businesses, causes, and products.
- Getting started is easy! Just click **Create a page**.

Local

- **Local** works much like Yelp. If you'd like general suggestions, browse the middle of the page. Recommended businesses are listed by category. Search at the top of the page for local reviews and recommendations.
- Want to write a review? Search for the location first. The business listing will have a pencil icon in the upper right-hand corner. Click this to write your review and set your star rating.

From *Teaching Social Media: The Can-Do Guide* by Liz Kirchhoff.
Santa Barbara, CA: Libraries Unlimited. Copyright © 2014.

Settings

- First, check out **Google+ Settings**.
- Start with **Who can interact with you and your posts. Who can send you notifications?** will let you choose how often you get notified about something.
  - **Anyone** means that you will get notified anytime anyone posts anything.
  - **Only you** will restrict these notifications so that you see only your own content.
  - If you like, you can choose **Custom**, which lets you decide which people you will see notifications from. You can view your notifications any time by clicking on the bell in the upper right-hand corner of the page.
  - **Who can comment on your public posts?** lets you determine who can comment on your freely available things. The options are essentially the same as above, from **Anyone** down to **Only you** or **Custom**.
- **Who can Hangout with you** lets you decide who you'd like to accept Hangout requests from. Click **Customize** to get a list of your circles. You'll be able to use the drop-down menus to adjust each circle. Getting too many notifications? Uncheck the box that says **Get notified about Hangout requests**.
- **Shared Endorsements** uses your reviews and recommendations in ads. If you would prefer to not allow this, click **Edit**, then scroll down the page until you see **Based on my activity, Google may show my name and profile photo in shared endorsements that appear in ads.** Uncheck the box and click **Save**. A popup box will appear to confirm. Click **Continue**. You can always return to this setting later to change it if you wish to do so.
- Click **Back to Account Settings** in the upper left-hand corner to return to the previous page.
- **Notification delivery** lets you choose whether you'd like to be notified by phone or email. You can include additional phone numbers and email addresses here, too.
- **Manage subscriptions** has two boxes to check if you'd like to be updated activity outside of your normal circles, or if you'd like Google+ news.
- **Receive notifications** lets you specify which updates you'd like to be notified about. By default, these are all checked. Just uncheck those you don't need updates about.
- **Google+ Pages** acts as a shortcut to add a page once you've searched Google with a "+" (plus sign) and a company name. Check the box if you'd like to add this feature.
- **Apps & activities** lets you manage any apps you use within Google. To use it, click **Manage apps & activities**. You probably won't have anything to manage yet, so you can return to this setting later.
- **Your circles** allows you to set the default for who automatically sees content that you share. Click **Customize** if you'd like to edit the Google+ default.
- **Accessibility** is a great option for people with visual impairment. It changes the layout of the page so that it's easier to read. Check the box if you'd like to use this feature.

From *Teaching Social Media: The Can-Do Guide* by Liz Kirchhoff.
Santa Barbara, CA: Libraries Unlimited. Copyright © 2014.

- The next section deals with how your **Photos** are managed. Check the box in front of each option you'd like to use. Note that this section also tells you how much storage space you've used. Google+ gives you 15 GB of space. If you use that much and would like more, you may purchase it.
- **Google Drive**, formerly Google Docs, is a great place to store documents, slideshows, and photos. This next option allows you to check a box if you'd like Google+ to add those images to your library. This only makes them more easily available to you, and doesn't automatically share them.
- **Auto Enhance** color corrects your photos. Select the appropriate checkbox for how much you'd like Google+ to apply this tool.
- **Auto Awesome** combines your photos into animations or group pictures. This is on by default. If you'd like to turn it off, uncheck the box.
- Under **Auto Awesome**, you'll see an option to auto-approve tags by a particular group. When someone from this circle tags you, it automatically appears on your profile. To change this, just click the X next to the name of the circle. If you'd like to add a circle or individuals to this setting, click **+Add more people.**
- **Profile** offers a series of options to determine the visibility of some elements of your profile. Take a moment now to read through these and select those you'd like to activate.
- **Hashtags** automatically adds searchable words from Google to your posts. This helps make your posts easier to find.
- **Location Settings** should be currently unchecked. If you choose to turn this feature on, it will work a bit like Foursquare. Your places will then be visible to your circles.
- Finally, if you decide that Google+ isn't for you, you can delete your profile under **Disable Google+.**
- If you choose to do so, there are several more sets of privacy controls within Google. Because they aren't specifically for Google+, we won't cover them here, but if you would like to review them, look for their category listings on the left-hand side of the page.

Terms

- **Circles:** Groups of friends that can be organized in any way.
- **Stream:** Where the updates of your friends appear.
- **Hangouts:** Video chats with your friends.
- **Hangouts on Air:** Hangouts that are live streamed and saved to YouTube.

Resources

- **Mashable Google+ Guide:** http://mashable.com/category/google-plus/
- **Google+ Help:** https://support.google.com/plus/?hl=en#topic=3049661

CHAPTER 8

Other Social Media

No one book can cover all the social media out there. This book covers in depth those that librarians get asked about the most as well as those that are already widely taught. In this chapter, you'll take a look at other social media websites and apps that would make great classes. You'll get an overview of the service, learn how it's used and features you might like to cover in class, explore different versions of the class that you might teach, and discuss which services it might pair well with. While this is by no means a comprehensive list, it will hopefully give you some ideas for future classes.

GOODREADS

What It Is

Goodreads is a website and app that helps users track what they're reading, share with friends, and get recommendations for their next read. With over 20 million members, there are lots of people to share what you're reading with, and many ways to discover that next great book. Now that Goodreads has been acquired by Amazon, you can expect deep Amazon and Kindle integration with the Goodreads service. This should make it easier to rate books and get suggestions right from your device.

How It Can Be Used

People use Goodreads in many different ways. Some users find it works best as a simple catalog of what they have read and what they'd like to read next. Some people love to write reviews, and use the site to comment and track the books they've loved and hated. Others use the forums to find new books or to identify books that they read long ago. Still others love the access that Goodreads provides to authors. The Goodreads Reading Challenge is also a huge draw, attracting more and more people annually. Every January, members choose a reading goal for the year. Progress toward the goal is tracked on the sidebar of the website.

What to Cover

Goodreads is an easy website and app to use. The design is fairly intuitive, so your students will probably only need a bit of help to get started. Show them the basics of setting up an account, including how to start logging their books. Spend some time on searching for books, as well as using the member database to find new (and current!) friends. Focus on the **Recent Updates** page, where your students can see what their friends are reading and reviewing. They can **Like** or **Comment** on anything on this page, and if they see something interesting, they can add it to their **Want to Read** shelf. Have them take a look at the **discussions** tab, since there they'll find the forums. **Recommendations** generates ideas for new titles to read based on titles from their shelves and popular books on Amazon and Goodreads. Finally, ask students to take a look at their settings. Here they can connect their profile to Facebook or Twitter, change their passwords, set privacy controls, and delete their accounts.

Versions of This Class

Teaching Goodreads shouldn't take long, and you'll have plenty of time to talk about other services. You can pair Goodreads with other social book sites like LibraryThing or Shelfari (also owned by Amazon). You might create a class that caters specifically to book clubs, covering several of these social sites along with one for finding new members (try Reader's Circle or Meetup for this). You could also throw in LitLovers and Reading Group Guides for discussion questions and reading guides, and do a quick demo on how to contact authors via Facebook or Twitter.

If you have lots of aspiring authors in your area, consider teaching a class on how to become a Goodreads author and to enhance your presence on social book sites. Finally, you could teach Goodreads with some fanfiction and authorial sites like WattPad. More and more major authors are getting their start on these kinds of sites, so this approach could be really appealing.

As far as community partners go, this is a great opportunity to partner with book clubs in your area. Writers groups would also be a good choice.

MYFITNESSPAL

What It Is

MyFitnessPal is one of many diet and fitness trackers on the market right now. The goal of these types of websites and apps is to make accurate calorie and fitness tracking easy while connecting you to a network of like-minded individuals for support and encouragement. As one of the largest tracking websites and apps, MyFitnessPal boasts a large catalog of food and exercise to make tracking fast and easy.

How It Can Be Used

Many people use the MyFitnessPal app or website strictly for inputting and tracking calories and exercise. The app is especially helpful for this, since it tracks your goals and history. It also breaks down specific nutritional macros, helping you to determine whether you are meeting your nutritional goals for the day. It has a really useful barcode scanner that connects to the food catalog, meaning that adding in foods can take just a few seconds. MyFitnessPal also partners with a number of other fitness applications. Once you connect the two accounts, you can use an app like Runtastic or Striiv to track your daily steps or your running session. At the end of the day, this syncs with MyFitnessPal. This is more accurate and saves time and hassle.

Other users really enjoy MyFitnessPal for its social aspects. In many ways, this is the Facebook of the fitness world. You can post statuses and comment on the activity of others. If you are comfortable doing so, you can allow the app and website to display notifications to your followers every time you complete your food diary, lose weight, or exercise. These are settings that are completely determined by the user, so all can be absolutely private if you choose to make them so. It's important to note that MyFitnessPal will *never* display your weight—only what you've lost.

What to Cover

With a website that tracks such personal information as this, it is paramount to explore the settings. As the instructor, you'll want to make sure that everyone is comfortable with establishing and changing the settings. Since a huge portion of the users of this service work almost exclusively with the app, be sure to show your students the basics of food logging, weighing in, writing statuses, and interacting with others. Show the class the many applications that can work with MyFitnessPal, found under **Apps & Devices**. If any of your students have a FitBit or Jawbone, these also can easily sync to MyFitnessPal.

Versions of This Class

MyFitnessPal works great in classes on how to use these tools to get fit for the New Year. Consider teaching a demonstration-style class with a number of options for tracking. Other great food trackers include MyNetDiary, FitDay, Lose It!, My Daily Plate, and SparkPeople. Fitness and activity trackers include Moves, Runtastic, Runtastic Pedometer, RunKeeper, Nike+Running, and tons more.

You may want to co-teach this class with your local gym or community fitness center. Perhaps they'd even be willing to provide a free trial for attendees. Many gyms provide free trials already, so it's not much of a stretch.

TRIPADVISOR

What It Is

TripAdvisor is a terrific website and app for travelers who are looking for honest reviews, photos, and complete information on hotels, resorts, services, and much more. Reviews are submitted by actual travelers and can help planners determine where to go, what to do, and what to avoid while on their trip. TripAdvisor can be the cornerstone of a great class on trip planning.

How It Can Be Used

TripAdvisor is best used while planning each stage of a trip. It's a particularly useful way to find a great hotel. It's also great for use while traveling to vet tours, restaurants, and other travel activities.

What to Cover

This is a really intuitive website with a layout that should be familiar to many. There's no need to make an account to search (only to post reviews), so there's no need to spend time talking about profiles or privacy. Instead, focus your class on searching TripAdvisor for reviews. Pick out a few hotels, a tour group, and a few local restaurants and demonstrate how to search and vet the reviews that are retrieved. Show your class how to sort reviews by rating and how to read for area recommendations. For example, many reviews for hotels mention great restaurants nearby or particularly positive recommendations for tour guides.

Versions of This Class

As an instructor, I've taught TripAdvisor a number of times as part of a "Plan Your Trip Online" class. I also cover the useful Travelzoo for awesome trip deals, Airbnb and CouchSurfing for nontraditional places to stay, Yelp for great reviews, Foursquare for city guides, and even Google Drive for creating an itinerary that can be edited and shared by anyone you'd like to give access to. No trip class would be complete without TripIt, a useful itinerary and trip planner. When you create your account on TripIt, you're given an email address. As you get each confirmation for your trip (flight, hotel, tours, etc.), you forward these emails to the address you were given. TripIt uses these to build an itinerary for you that includes your plans, your flight information and status, maps of the area you're in, confirmation numbers, and lots more. The app is connected to your account, so you have all of your travel information handy whether you are near your computer or not.

Frequently, students in this class are seniors. Consider teaching this at a retirement community or at your local senior center.

REDDIT

What It Is

Reddit is an influential, massive online message board. Users post text and image links to "subreddits," or boards devoted to specific categories and topics. The power in Reddit lies in the incredibly diverse variety of topics that it covers, most with their own subreddits. Reddit users are some of the most engaged online, and most subreddits are very active. It's a great place to start if you're researching something like a new diet or an exercise routine. There are terrific Reddits for travel, news, cities, humor, questions, technology, music, photography, philanthropy, and much more.

Reddit is simple to use. Redditors (or Reddit Editors—this can be anyone who has an account) post an article, text message, or image in a subreddit. Readers can comment, upvote, and downvote. The most upvoted items rise to the top of the subreddit, naturally filtering the good from the bad. The posts and comments with the most upvotes land on the Front Page, where they are seen by the Reddit community at large. Comments can be upvoted or downvoted, too. An upvote (and a post or comment) is good for one point. A downvote subtracts a point. Reddit users can view this post and comment karma. A Redditor with lots of points tends to be more influential (although sometimes they're just more active) than those with few points.

How It Can Be Used

Reddit is often referred to as the "front page" of the Internet. That's an apt description! Many people use Reddit as a way to keep up with what's new in the world, trending articles, new memes, and viral videos. Others use it as a message board for questions and answers on particular topics.

Lots of great activism work and philanthropic causes gain huge amounts of attention due to Reddit.

What to Cover

In this class, talk about what Reddit is and how to create an account (users don't need an account to read Reddit, but they will need an account to post, comment, upvote, or downvote). Show your students how to search for subreddits, how to post comments, and how to upvote and downvote comments and posts. As part of your class, be sure to also demonstrate how to use Imgur and Tumblr, since those two services are used to post pictures on Reddit. Talk a bit about the Front Page, too, as that can be an excellent way to find great new subreddits.

Also consider talking a bit about mobile apps for Reddit. The most widely used seems to be Alien Blue. Using Reddit on Alien Blue is slightly different from using the website, so a short tutorial would be helpful.

Finally, be sure to note that as awesome as Reddit is, it is full of swear words and other potentially offensive content. Mitigate this by vetting the subreddits you show ahead of time. Warn the class that you can't control what they might see before you start. Many posts that are potentially offensive carry a red NSFW (Not Safe For Work) tag, so watch for those, too.

Here is a short list of great subreddits to show during your class:
- ELI5 (Explain Like I'm Five): Redditors ask users to explain complex ideas simply
- Travel: gorgeous photos, recommendations, travel questions, and stories
- Aww: puppies, kittens, and anything else that's cute
- AdviceAnimals: this is where lots of popular memes start out
- Bestof: the best Reddit content
- IAmA: Experts in various fields post soliciting questions; lots of authors here, too
- Science: Anything and everything science related
- Worldnews: Articles from around the world
- Todayilearned: Interesting and random facts, usually with linked articles so you can learn more
- AskReddit: Open-ended questions intended to start a discussion. Many of these are of the "Tell us about a time when you ..." variety.
- Pics: Images of all kinds. Watch for the NSFW tags!
- Funny: Jokes, silly pictures, funny articles

Versions of This Class

Reddit is a rich enough site that it could stand alone as a class, but if you'd like to teach it with some other services, consider teaching an Internet discovery class. Reddit would be great to teach with StumbleUpon, Digg, and Alltop.

TUMBLR

What It Is

Tumblr is a microblogging website and app that is mostly comprised of images, GIFs, and video. Like Twitter, posts tend to be extremely brief. With more than 150 million blogs, Tumblr is a major force in social networking and the blogging world.

Tumblr is simple and easy to use. Bloggers use a dashboard to upload photos and video and add captions. Posts can be live immediately, or scheduled for release later. Like many other social media sites, Tumblr uses tags for posts to help viewers search for and find new content.

If you don't have a Tumblr account but would like to follow specific Tumblrs, just add the RSS feed to your reader of choice.

How It Can Be Used

Tumblr is entertaining and lots of fun to use, but it's also useful. It's a natural platform for photographers, videographers, and visual artists of all kinds. It's a great way to share travel and family photos, too.

What to Cover

Tumblr is fairly simple to use and to teach. Start by showing some great Tumblr examples, such as the ones on the following list. Then demonstrate how to set up an account and how to navigate the dashboard. It would be appropriate to spend a bit of time discussing fair use here, since much of the content on Tumblr is re-blogged from other sources. Finally, show your students how to find and follow other Tumblrs.

Here is a short list of Tumblrs you might show your class:
- Reasons My Son Is Crying: A hilarious Tumblr with photos of kids crying from around the world. Parents submit these with a short description of the irrational reason why their kid is upset.
- How Do I Put This Gently?: Sometimes NSFW blog of gifs from around the Internet.
- Natgeofound: Gorgeous and unique photography from National Geographic.
- T-Rex Trying: The unfortunate escapades of T-Rex, told in cartoons.
- Humans of New York: With portraits and personal stories, this Tumblr celebrates the diversity of a big city.

- Postcards from America: Photography from a group of artists that focuses on one city at a time.
- Raise Our Story: A series of stories and photographs of undocumented youth in the United States.

Versions of This Class

Tumblr is a natural companion to other services. Teach it with Twitter and Vine in a microblogging class. Add in Blogger and WordPress for a more general class on blogging. Want to focus on multimedia? Teach it with Instagram, Flickr, and Imgur.

RAVELRY

What It Is

Ravelry is a site for knitters and crocheters to share projects, patterns, and finished projects. Users have notebooks, forums, and lots of other tools to inspire and organize. The site is not only useful—it's beautiful and extremely social, too.

How It Can Be Used

Ravelry is great for people who love fiber arts. You can catalog yarns, find and save patterns, ask for advice, watch instructional videos, and lots more. Users and companies can even sell fiber, patterns, and finished products.

What to Cover

In this class, cover how to set up an account as well as how to add patterns, pictures, and things that inspire you to your notebooks. Be sure to spend some time demonstrating the use of the forums, including posting and commenting.

Versions of This Class

Ravelry is fairly easy to use, so it shouldn't take long to teach. Luckily, there are many other services to teach it with. Consider teaching it with a "crafty commerce" class. Start with Ravelry, then discuss setting up a store and selling on Etsy and eBay. For students who'd simply like to learn more about crafting without selling, consider teaching Ravelry with Etsy (a terrific place to buy interesting and unusual patterns), YouTube for great how-to videos, and Reddit for outstanding crafting subreddits.

Consider teaching this class at a local fiber or yarn store or a textile school, if you have one nearby. Invite your area stitching clubs, and pair it with a stitching session or expert demonstration for a really fun class. You might also use it in teaching a commerce class with a local small business expert.

PANDORA INTERNET RADIO

What It Is

Pandora is an online streaming radio service that is used for music discovery. Users can have multiple stations, each of which is started by typing a song or artist. Pandora is based on the Music Genome Project, which identifies hundreds of characteristics of thousands of songs. The service uses these characteristics to identify and play similar songs. Listeners can give a song a thumbs-up or a thumbs-down. A thumbs-up means that the song will be added to a list of music that will be played again. Pandora uses these selections as a way to find even more music for you. Giving a song a thumbs-down means that it won't be played again. Users can also skip songs if they wish. There is a paid version of Pandora, but most people use the free, ad-supported service.

How It Can Be Used

Pandora is obviously great radio, since it's based entirely on the taste of the user. Beyond that, it works as an excellent music discovery tool. In many ways, Pandora has leveled the playing field for small artists. Pandora seems to give equal playing time to indie artists as well as giants of the music industry. Because of this, users get exposed to artists they never would have heard otherwise.

What to Cover

Teaching Pandora shouldn't really take more than a few minutes. Just show your patrons how to set up an account, start a station, and use the recommendation tools (thumbs-up and thumbs-down, as well as skip). Demonstrate how to create multiple stations, and show the class the setting for skipping a song you like, but are just tired of. You might also take a few minutes to demonstrate the app. It's widely used and is a cinch.

Versions of This Class

I've often taught Pandora as part of a web media class. Include several other streaming radio services (like last.fm, Spotify, or Rdio) as well as

YouTube and Instagram. If your library has them, this is the perfect time to mention and demonstrate Hoopla, Zinio, Freegal, Overdrive, 3M, and more. It's a fun class, and students almost always recommend other services they enjoy.

PREZI

What It Is

Prezi is a great way to liven up a PowerPoint presentation. Slides are laid out on a background in groups, allowing users to easily group them into concepts that can enhance a presentation. PowerPoint slides can be uploaded into a Prezi, or an entire project can be created with the editor. Many people can collaborate on the same Prezi, making group presentations easy. Finally, there's a Prezi viewer available for iPad. Presenters just plug the iPad into the projector, and they're ready to go.

How It Can Be Used

Prezis are used for school presentations as well as for business purposes. They offer you a great way to pitch a new idea or product and are especially good for presenting complex or complicated ideas. The free version is a great alternative to PowerPoint.

What to Cover

In this class, cover account creation and other basics. Discuss uploading images and video, demonstrate the editing tools, and show some successful Prezis. You'll probably also want to demonstrate the Prezi viewing app for the iPad, since this can be a real selling feature for this service.

Versions of This Class

Consider teaching Prezi as part of a class of social media tools for businesses. You could even partner with your local Chamber of Commerce for a class like this. Consider teaching it with Twitter, Facebook, and some productivity tools like Evernote or Drive.

GOOGLE DRIVE

What Is It

Google Drive (formerly Google Docs) is a useful tool that lets you work on just about any type of document online. Files can be opened anywhere with an Internet connection and can be shared with as many people as you'd like. Multiple users can work on a file at the same time, making it a great tool for collaboration. Drive is also a great way to help you access your files from anywhere. Most file formats can be uploaded onto Drive, and you can download those same files in nearly any format, too. This helps to get rid of file format problems.

How It Can Be Used

How can't it be used? Drive does just about everything that Office does, so it can easily replace that product, especially on devices that don't have it (think iPads and other tablets). You can use it as a word processing tool (this book was written primarily in Drive), as a way to share and edit a spreadsheet, as a PowerPoint alternative, and much more. Because file size limits are so high, it's a great way to back up some of your important documents, too.

What to Cover

In this class, describe how to set up Google accounts (if your patrons have Gmail, they can use those accounts to access Drive). Discuss the different types of files that can be uploaded and downloaded as well as how to create new files. Spend some time talking about file management and folders, too. Since one of the strongest features of Drive is collaboration, show your students how to share files; and invite others to view and edit work.

Versions of This Class

Consider teaching Drive as part of a class on device file management. As increasing numbers of people start using iPads and tablets, we seem to get more questions about how to do spreadsheets and documents. Pair Drive with other productivity services like Evernote and Dropbox, as well as discussing other services like online Office. Spend some time on the apps for these services, as that version of the service can be very different from the online version.

Conclusion

TAILORING CLASSES TO YOUR COMMUNITY

The best way to tailor classes for your community is to look around and evaluate where there are needs and gaps. How can you add value? First, think about where you actually teach. For example, consider the earlier suggestion for teaching Ravelry in a fiber shop. Your class will be more interesting if it's held in a place full of supplies that people enjoy seeing and may wish to purchase. It's an obvious plus for the shop, since they'll probably sell more with you there.

Consider the combination of classes you teach, or the slant that you teach them with. If you have a lot of business owners in your area, how can you tailor your stock classes to make them attractive? Can you co-teach them with your local Chamber of Commerce?

Perhaps your community is really struggling with the downturn in employment. If this is the case, consider teaching LinkedIn along with resume assistance and drop-in sessions. There are many community organizations that would make great partners in this. Making this connection helps your patrons and strengthens your connections within your community.

The bottom line here is that you know your community best. Think about what they need most, and take your classes from there. Your classes and outreach may not always work out the first time. If they don't, evaluate why not and try again.

EVALUATING YOUR SUCCESSES

The easiest way to evaluate how you did is to ask! Some libraries have written forms for this, but I've always just preferred to ask for feedback. Of course, many people will be too polite to tell you, but you can look for nonverbal cues to tell you how you did. Is your class engaged? What did they ask lots of questions about? Did they have trouble keeping up with you? Pay attention to your students while you are teaching, and mentally note all of the feedback you're getting. Jot down your observations after class. As you prepare for your next class, use this information to do better.

Another thing to pay attention to is how many people approach you for one-on-one appointments, and what questions they are asking. If you're getting the same questions over and over, it's a pretty clear sign that you need to spend more time on that concept in class.

If you're feeling brave, you might consider taking a few minutes at the end of class to ask for feedback. Ask some questions. Did everyone understand what you were talking about? Was the pace okay? Did they get what they needed? What other classes would they like to take? Your classes should really be more of a conversation than a lecture, so this should be a natural extension of that.

TEACHING MORE EFFECTIVELY AND REMAINING RELEVANT

By asking for feedback and listening to what your students say, you'll be well on your way to being a better teacher. Keep a dialog going with your students, and reevaluate your classes and your teaching style. Don't be afraid to try new things!

As far as remaining relevant, this is an ongoing task. As discussed earlier, you need to constantly scan your environment for information and cues. What is Facebook doing these days? Has anything changed? What's new in social networking? What are you getting asked about? What are some big, important issues in your community? Where do you see a need? Is there a group or business nearby that might be willing to be partners? Keep asking yourself these things, and you'll keep getting new ideas to improve what you're doing and how it's done. It is this inquisitiveness and responsiveness that will help you become and stay a great instructor.

INDEX

Account settings: Facebook, 53; LinkedIn, 80; Pinterest, 34–35; Twitter, 9. *See also* Settings

Account set up: Foursquare, 17–18; Google+, 89; Pinterest, 31–32; Twitter, reluctance to, 2; Yelp, 23–24

Adding connections, LinkedIn, 77

Adding content to profile, LinkedIn, 73–74

Additional info, LinkedIn, 75

Ads, Facebook, 58–59

Airbnb, 107

Amazon, 103

Apps, Facebook, 50

Background, LinkedIn, 74–75

Bells and whistles, Twitter, 7–8

Blocking, Facebook, 56

Blogging: micro, 1, 4, 10; sites (*See* specific types)

Boards, Pinterest, 34–35

Business Twitter, 3–4

Chat, Facebook, 60

Class variations: Foursquare, 16; Goodreads, 104; Google+, 88; Google Drive, 113; LinkedIn, 72; MyFitnessPal, 106; Pandora, 111–12; Prezi, 112; Ravelry, 110–11; Reddit, 108–9; TripAdvisor, 106–7; Tumblr, 110; Twitter, 3–4; Yelp, 22

Communities, Google+, 92–93

Completing profile, LinkedIn, 76

Concerns and questions. *See* Questions and concerns

Connections, LinkedIn, 76, 77, 78

CouchSurfing, 107

Cover page, Facebook, 44–45

Creating account. *See* Account set up

Creating original Pin, Pinterest, 34

DMs (Direct Messages), 1

Editing profile, Facebook, 47–48

Education, LinkedIn, 75

Essentials: Facebook, 61–65;
    Foursquare, 20; Google+,
    97–101; LinkedIn, 82–86;
    Pinterest, 36–37; Twitter,
    10–12; Yelp, 26–27
Etsy, 110
Events: Facebook, 49–50;
    Google+, 93
Experience, LinkedIn, 75
Expertise and skills, LinkedIn, 75
Exploring page, Facebook, 44

Facebook: additional settings, 59;
    ads, 58–59; apps, 50, 57–58;
    blocking, 56; chat, 60; common
    problems in class, 41; cover page,
    44–45; description, 43; editing
    profile, 47–48; essentials, 61–65;
    events, 49–50; exploring page,
    44; find friends, 50; followers,
    57; friends, 47, 51; general
    account settings, 53; getting
    started, 44; groups, 50–51; how
    to prepare, 39–41; instructor
    notes, 42–60; managing photos,
    45–47; messages, 49; mobile, 57;
    More tab, 47; navigation bar, 51;
    news feed, 48–49; notifications,
    52; notification settings, 57;
    overview, 39; pages, 51;
    payments, 59; possible
    variations, 41; privacy settings,
    53, 54–55, 66–70; search, 51–52;
    security settings, 53–54;
    shortcuts, 52; special
    considerations, 41–42; support
    dashboard, 59; teaching script
    for, 42–43; timeline and tagging,
    55–56; using, 43–44
Find alumni, LinkedIn, 77–78
Finding friends: Facebook, 50;
    Google+, 89
Finding Pin source, Pinterest, 33
FitBit, 105

FitDay, 106
Followers, Facebook, 57
Following: LinkedIn, 76; others,
    Twitter, 6; trends, Twitter, 7
Foursquare, 107; class variations,
    16; creating account, 17–18;
    description, 17; essentials, 20; how
    to prepare, 15–16; instructor notes,
    17–19; overview, 15; questions and
    concerns, 16; searching, 19;
    teaching script for, 17; using, 18
Friends, Facebook, 47, 51;
    finding, 50

General account settings,
    Facebook, 53
Getting started. See Starting out
Goodreads: class variations, 104;
    description, 103; teaching script
    for, 104; using, 103–4
Goodreads Reading Challenge, 104
Google+: class variations, 88;
    closing, 96; communities, 92–93;
    description, 87; essentials,
    97–101; events, 93; finding
    friends, 89; getting started, 88;
    hangouts, 93–94; home page, 89;
    how to prepare, 87; instructor
    notes, 88–96; local, 94; pages,
    94; people, 90; photos, 91–92;
    profile, 89–90; questions and
    concerns, 87–88; settings, 94–96;
    setting up account, 89; teaching
    script for, 88; what's hot, 92
Google Docs. See Google Drive
Google Drive, 107; class variations,
    113; description, 112–13; teaching
    script for, 113; using, 113
Groups: Facebook, 50–51;
    LinkedIn, 76

Hangouts, Google+, 93–94
Help center, LinkedIn, 80
Home page, Google+, 89

Instructor notes: Facebook, 42–60; Foursquare, 17–19; Google+, 88–96; LinkedIn, 72–81; Pinterest, 30–35; Twitter, 4–5; Yelp, 22–25
Interests, LinkedIn, 78–79

Jawbone, 105
Jobs, LinkedIn, 78

Kindle, 103

LinkedIn: account navigation bar, 79; adding connections, 77; adding content to profile, 73–74; additional info, 75; background, 74–75; closing, 81; completing profile, 76; connections, 76, 77; description, 73; education, 75; essentials, 82–86; experience, 75; find alumni, 77–78; following, 76; groups, 76; help center, 80; how to prepare, 71; instructor notes, 72–81; interests, 78–79; jobs, 78; note on adding connections, 78; possible variations, 72; privacy and settings, 80; profile and account settings, 80; questions and concerns, 72; skills and expertise, 75; special considerations, 72; starting out, 73; teaching script for, 72–73; viewing your public profile, 74; who's viewed your profile, 76–77
Local, Google+, 94
Lose It!, 106

Managing photos: Facebook, 45–47; Google+, 91–92
Messages, Facebook, 49
Micro blogging, 1, 4, 10
Mobile Facebook, 57
More tab, Facebook, 47

Music Genome Project, 111
My Daily Plate, 106
MyFitnessPal: class variations, 106; description, 105; teaching script for, 105; using, 105
MyNetDiary, 106

Navigation bar: Facebook, 51; LinkedIn, 79; Pinterest, 33–34; Twitter, 8
News feed, Facebook, 48–49
Note on adding connections, LinkedIn, 78
Notifications, Facebook, 52; settings, 57

Organizing, Twitter, 9

Pages: exploration, Facebook, 44; Facebook, 51; Google+, 94
Pandora: class variations, 111–12; description, 111; teaching script for, 111; using, 111
Payments, Facebook, 59
People, Google+, 90
Photos managing: Facebook, 45–47; Google+, 91–92
Pinning, Pinterest, 32
Pins, Pinterest, 34–35
Pinterest: account settings, 34–35; boards, 34–35; creating account, 31–32; creating original Pin, 34; description, 30–31; essentials, 36–37; finding Pin source, 33; how to prepare, 29; instructor notes, 30–35; navigation and searching, 33–34; other options, 33; overview, 29; Pinning, 32; Pins, 34–35; possible variations, 30; questions and concerns, 29–30; special considerations, 30; teaching script for, 30; using, 32
Posting videos, Twitter, 6

PowerPoint, 15, 40, 112, 113. *See also* Prezi

Preparing: Facebook, 39–41; Foursquare, 15–16; Google+, 87; LinkedIn, 71; Pinterest, 29; Twitter, 1–2; Yelp, 21

Prezi: class variations, 112; description, 112; teaching script for, 112; using, 112

Privacy concerns: Facebook, 53, 54–55, 66–70; LinkedIn, 80; Twitter, 2–3. *See also* Security concerns

Profile(s): adding content to, LinkedIn, 73–74; completing, LinkedIn, 76; editing, Facebook, 47–48; Google+, 89–90; settings, LinkedIn, 80; viewing your public, LinkedIn, 74; who's viewed your, LinkedIn, 76–77

Questions and concerns: Foursquare, 16; Google+, 87–88; LinkedIn, 72; Pinterest, 29–30; Twitter, 2–3; Yelp, 21–22

Ravelry: class variations, 110–11; description, 110; teaching script for, 110; using, 110

Reddit: class variations, 108–9; description, 107; teaching script for, 108; using, 107–8

Reddit Editors, 107

Redditors, 107

Responding, Twitter, 7

RSS feed, 109

Runtastic, 105

Search/searching: Facebook, 51–52; Foursquare, 19; Pinterest, 33–34

Security concerns: Facebook, 53–54; Twitter, 2–3. *See also* Privacy concerns

Settings: account, Pinterest, 34–35; additional, Facebook, 59; general account, Facebook, 53; Google+, 94–96; notification, Facebook, 57; privacy, Facebook, 53, 54–55, 66–70; privacy and, LinkedIn, 80; profile and account, LinkedIn, 80; security, Facebook, 53–54; Twitter, 9. *See also* Account settings; specific settings

Sharing, Twitter, 7

Shortcuts: Facebook, 52; Twitter, 9

Signing out, Twitter, 9

Skills and expertise, LinkedIn, 75

SparkPeople, 106

Special considerations: Facebook, 41–42; LinkedIn, 72; Pinterest, 30

Starting out: Facebook, 44; Google+, 88; LinkedIn, 73; Twitter, 5–6

Striiv, 105

Support dashboard, Facebook, 59

Tagging, Facebook, 55–56

Teaching script: for Facebook, 42–43; for Foursquare, 17; for Goodreads, 104; for Google+, 88; for Google Drive, 113; for LinkedIn, 72–73; for MyFitnessPal, 105; for Pandora, 111; for Pinterest, 30; for Prezi, 112; for Ravelry, 110; for Reddit, 108; for TripAdvisor, 106; for Tumblr, 109–10; for Twitter, 4; for Yelp, 22

Timeline, Facebook, 55–56

Tools, Yelp, 24–25

Travelzoo, 106

TripAdvisor: class variations, 106–7; description, 106; teaching script for, 106; using, 106

TripIt, 107

Tumblr: class variations, 110;
  description, 109; teaching script
  for, 109–10; using, 109
Tweeting, Twitter, 6
Twitter: bells and whistles, 7–8; for
  business, 3–4; class variations,
  3–4; essentials, 10–12; following
  others, 6; following trends, 7;
  how to prepare, 1–2; how to
  tweet, 6; instructor notes, 4–5;
  organizing, 9; overview, 1;
  posting videos, 6; privacy and
  security concerns, 2–3; purpose
  of, 2, 4–5; reluctance to create
  account, 2; responding and
  sharing, 7; searching, 8–9;
  settings, 9; shortcuts, 9; signing
  out, 9; starting out, 5–6; teaching
  script for, 4; usage, 5–9; using
  navigation bar, 8

Video posting, Twitter, 6
Viewing your public profile,
  LinkedIn, 74

WattPad, 104
What's hot, Google+, 92
Whistles and bells, Twitter, 7–8
Who's viewed your profile,
  LinkedIn, 76–77
Writing first review, Yelp, 24

Yelp: class variations, 22; creating
  account, 23–24; description, 22;
  essentials, 26–27; evaluating
  reviews, 23; how to prepare, 21;
  instructor notes, 22–25; more
  tools, 24–25; overview, 21;
  questions and concerns, 21–22;
  teaching script for, 22; using, 23;
  writing first review, 24